SUNLIGHT FOR CLOUDY DAYS

SUNLIGHT
FOR CLOUDY
DAYS

Fourteen Vital and Moving Topics from
C. H. Spurgeon

THE WAKEMAN TRUST, LONDON

SUNLIGHT FOR CLOUDY DAYS
© Wakeman, 2010

THE WAKEMAN TRUST
(Wakeman Trust is a UK Registered Charity)

UK Registered Office
38 Walcot Square
London SE11 4TZ

USA Office
300 Artino Drive
Oberlin, OH 44074-1263
Website: www.wakemantrust.org

ISBN 978 1 870855 67 9

Cover design by Andrew Owen

Printed by Stephens & George, Merthyr Tydfil, UK

Contents

These chapters consist of
prayer meeting addresses, sermons and shorter
items of C. H. Spurgeon, abridged and edited over recent
years for the *Sword & Trowel* magazine
(founded by Spurgeon in 1865).

Editor: Dr Peter Masters

1
Sunlight for Cloudy Days
When Humility Brings Assurance

'But I am poor and needy; yet the Lord thinketh upon me' *(Psalm 40.17)*.

NOT ALL PEOPLE will apply to themselves the first part of this text. Most churchgoers will accept it because it happens to be scriptural language, and yet we might not spontaneously say about ourselves, 'I am poor and needy.' Some even believe the opposite; for they have enough of this world's goods, and as for spiritual matters, they are strong and self-reliant. This is vainglory, and in the long run will end in vanity, and vexation of spirit, for if a person can do without God, it is certain that God can do without him, and the day will come when God *will* do without him, according to his word, 'I will ease me of mine adversaries.' Whoever has tried throughout life to do without God will inherit remorse for ever.

Yet there are some who cry, 'I am certainly poor and needy, but the Lord does not think of me. I have looked up to Heaven, but no eye of pity looks down upon me in my misery.' Many an afflicted mind, many a bereaved spirit, and many a downcast heart, has cried, 'The Lord counts the number of the stars, and calls them by their names; but, as for me, I cannot believe that he thinks upon me.' Dear friend, I hope you will be converted from this unbelief. I pray that you may not only be able to join in one half of this text by saying, 'I am poor and needy,' but that you may also unite in the second declaration, 'Yet the Lord thinketh upon me.' Whatever your insignificance and unworthiness, you may yet learn that the Lord has thoughts of love towards you, and is causing all things to work together for your external, internal, and eternal good.

Do not be surprised that David, the psalmist, should say, 'I am poor and needy; yet the Lord thinketh upon me,' for God's thoughts have often been with poor and needy persons. Look at Joseph when he was in prison, and the iron entered into his soul. His character was destroyed, and he was reproached, and punished unjustly. Yet we read that the Lord was with him, and in due time brought him out, and set him on the throne of Egypt.

So Ruth, the Moabitess, came penniless to Israel's land, and she went to glean among the sheaves as a poor, needy peasant woman. But the Lord was thinking upon her, and provided for her so greatly that she rose to honourable estate, and her name is written among the progenitors of our Lord Jesus. To give you a later example, the apostles were poor fishermen, with their little boats, and well-worn nets, upon the lake of Galilee; yet the Lord looked upon them, making uneducated and uncultured men the pioneers of his kingdom. Never mind how poor and needy you are, you may yet be heirs of God, and joint heirs with Jesus Christ.

'Yes,' you may say, 'but my trouble is that I am poor as to anything like *goodness* in the sight of God. I feel so guilty, and so far from being what I ought to be.' Yet the Lord has thought often of such people as this. Look at the blessed Master sitting on the well at Sychar, talking with that wanton woman who had had five husbands. She was a woman whom none would honour, but the Saviour thought upon her. Remember, too, the thief dying upon the cross, hanging next to the Redeemer, with all his sins upon him, for he had been a thief, and probably a murderer also. His prayer, 'Lord, remember me,' touched the heart of Jesus and, 'To day shalt thou be with me in paradise' was the gracious response. The Lord thought on him; and yet there was never one more poor and needy of morality and righteousness than he.

Also, there was Saul of Tarsus, the persecutor, breathing out threatenings and slaughter against the church of God, but the Merciful One in Heaven, who saw his sin, thought on him with love, and said, 'Saul, Saul, why persecutest thou me?' Poverty of all merit, and need of all grace, do not prevent the Lord from thinking upon men and women. This fact is as clear as the sun in the heavens. However spiritually poor you may be, you may yet partake of the riches of his grace, and so become rich in faith. Indeed, none but consciously needy ones ever obtain the privilege of saying, 'yet the Lord thinketh upon me.'

I was troubled when I was seeking the Lord with the notion that I was so utterly insignificant that the Lord would never notice *me*. There is no reason for such a fear, since the Lord has thought upon very obscure people. Think of the Syro-Phoenician woman's daughter. What was her name? Do you know what sort of a girl she was? Can you speak of her subsequent history? She is quite unknown to fame, yet the Lord thought upon her and healed her.

That little daughter of Jairus, a child of twelve years of age – what could she do? Did she become a distinguished woman? What life work did she perform? She makes no impression upon the biblical record, yet the Lord thought upon her, and even restored her from the dead. The widow's son, who was being carried out of the city of Nain, what did he achieve? What post of honour did he occupy? What lofty path did he pursue? We know nothing of him except that the Lord thought upon him. Most of the people whom the

Lord Jesus thought upon in the days of his flesh were unknown to fame; and, for my part, I judge that the happiest are those who pass through life unknown of men, but known of God.

During the French Revolution a man of great influence escaped the guillotine, and when asked how it happened, he replied, 'I made myself of no reputation, and kept silence.' Do not, therefore, think that your being in the background is any hindrance to the Lord's thinking upon you. He cares nothing about the blare of trumpets, or the blaze of fame; but looks upon the meek and lowly, and finds out those that are of a broken spirit and of a contrite heart, and that tremble at his Word, and with these he deigns to dwell. May we be found among them!

My desire is to do four things, upon each of which I will comment very briefly. From the words of the text I desire, first, *to help your faith* to remember that if you are poor and needy, the Lord thinks upon you. Then I long *to enlarge your hope*; thirdly, *to inflame your love*; and fourthly, *to direct your life*.

First, let me *help your faith*. You say to yourself, 'I cannot understand why God should think of me.' Why not? 'Because I am so insignificant.' Let me ask you if there is anything in the world which is not little to God. You say, 'There is the world itself;' and I answer, that the earth which we think so large, is no more to God than a single grain of dust. The solar system, and all the other systems that make up the creation of God, are as nothing to the infinite Jehovah.

So great is the universe that the most elevated conception of the greatest mind has never compassed more than a fragment of it, yet God is infinitely beyond the whole of created existence! A human being must always be really greater than his own works, and certainly God must be infinitely greater than all that he has ever made. You reply that you expect him to think of the great ones of the earth. However, most of *them* think very little of him. The Lord gets the least worthy treatment from those who are ranked as rich and honourable. When we reach Heaven, we shall find few kings and princes, few of the learned and applauded, for God hath 'chosen the poor of this world rich in faith'.

Again, if it should seem to you difficult for God to think upon the poor and needy, I invite you to answer the question, 'Who needs God's thoughts most?' On the field of battle, after the combat, if a surgeon should be there to attend to the wounded, where will he go first? Of course, he will go to those whose gaping wounds have almost opened for them the gates of death. The slightly wounded he will leave until he has time. The Lord looks upon us according to our needs. Our urgent needs move his mercy, and he will go first to those who require him most. Do you need his grace more than anyone else? Then he will hasten at once to you. If I see a physician's carriage hurrying down the street, I feel certain that he is not driving to my door, for I am not dangerously ill. But if I know of one who has fallen very ill, or has been badly injured by an accident, I conclude that he is going to him. When the angel of mercy is made to fly very swiftly, you can be sure that he is speeding to one who is in urgent need of grace.

Remember, too, that *God has always dealt with men from that point of view.* When God made his roll of election, before the earth was, he chose them as fallen and undeserving, that he might lift them up, to the praise of the glory of his grace. His choice of men was never guided by anything good that he saw in them; as Paul says, 'For the children being not yet born, neither having done any good or evil, that the purpose of God according to election might stand, not of works, but of him that calleth.'

The decree still stands, 'I will have mercy on whom I will have mercy, and I will have compassion on whom I will have compassion.' The Lord of grace asks in his sovereignty, 'Shall I not do as I will with my own?' God views all people as guilty, and yet he chooses to himself a people in whom his grace shall be resplendent. Therefore do not conclude that he will pass you by because you are poor and needy in terms of righteousness. Did he lay down his life to redeem those who were not captives? Did he pour out his blood to cleanse those who were already clean? If we had not needed a great salvation, would the Beloved One of Heaven have stooped to the death of the cross that we might be saved? 'This is a faithful saying, and worthy of all acceptation, that Christ Jesus came into the world to save' – *the righteous?* – oh no, but 'to save sinners; of whom I am chief'. Stagger not at the grace of God to your own hurt, but say, 'Though I be spiritually poor and needy, yet the Lord thinketh upon me.'

Furthermore, the *gift of God the Holy Spirit* proves that God deals with the poor and needy. If we were strong and full of all spiritual forces we would not have needed the Spirit of God to quicken and regenerate us, and we should not have needed him to abide in us as our Teacher and Helper. Why, brethren, you cannot even pray without the Spirit of God. The Spirit is given to help your infirmity in prayer, because that infirmity most surely exists. The gift of the Spirit of God to men is a proof that God looks upon them as being poor and needy in spiritual things. Now, if you feel that you cannot pray, you cannot repent, you cannot believe, you cannot do anything good in your own strength, do not fret about that, but fly to God for strength. Say, 'I am poor and needy; but the gift of the Holy Spirit is an evidence that the Lord thinks upon me.'

Let me further say, to help your faith, that though you say you are very poor and needy spiritually, you are not alone in this, for *so are all God's saints*, and the better believers are, the more they feel their poverty and need. Boasters talk 'exceeding proudly' about their spiritual attainments; but the more they glory, the more vain is their glory. True saints are humble. In a company where certain people were displaying their spiritual attainments, it was noticed that one devout person remained silent. Eventually, a talkative man turned to him, and asked, 'Have you no sanctification?' He replied, 'I never had any to boast of, and I hope I never shall have.'

The more high in grace, the more low in self-esteem. Ask the man who has the most holiness what he thinks of himself, and he will be the first to lament that he has not yet reached the point which he desires. We are like those old-fashioned wine glasses which had no foot to them, so that they could not stand upon the table, but had to be held in the hand. When Jesus has us in his hand, we can be filled with the water of life; but out of his hand we cannot hold a drop, nor even stand. We are nothing at all without our All-in-all. 'I can do all things through Christ which strengtheneth me,' said one. 'Without me ye can do nothing,' is the true word of Christ to every branch of the living Vine. Now, if all God's saints say that they are nobodies, do not despair because *you* are a nobody. If all confess that they can do nothing without Christ, do not despond because *you* also can do nothing without him.

Let me here relate a story, which may cheer those who feel themselves to be so lacking that the Lord will not think upon them. The Lord looks upon those who feel their guilt, and a Saviour is on the lookout for sinners quite as much as sinners are on the lookout for a Saviour. I heard that a great English prince once went to visit a king of Spain. The prince was taken down to the galleys to see the men who were chained to the oars, doomed to be slaves for life. In honour of the prince's visit, the king of Spain promised that he would set free one of those men at the selection of the prince.

The prince went to one prisoner and said, 'My poor fellow, I am sorry to see you in this plight, how came you here?' 'Ah! sir,' he answered, 'false witnesses gave evidence against me; I am suffering wrongfully.' 'Indeed!' said the prince, and passed on to the next man. 'My poor fellow, I am sorry to see you here, how did it happen?' 'Sir, I certainly did wrong, but not to any great extent. I ought not to be here.' 'Indeed!' said the prince, and he went on to others who told him similar tales.

At last he came to one prisoner, who said, 'Sir, I am often thankful that I am here; for I am sorry to acknowledge that if I had received my due I should have been executed. I am certainly guilty of all that was laid to my charge, and my severest punishment is just.' The prince replied ingeniously to him, 'It is a pity that such a guilty wretch as you are should be chained among these innocent men, and therefore I will set you free.' You smile, but how you will smile if Christ Jesus does the same for you. Assuredly this is his manner. He passes by those who think highly of themselves and looks upon those who are self-condemned, and plead guilty before him. He came not to call the righteous, but sinners to repentance. He thinks upon the poor and needy.

I ask you to look at the text again, by way of *enlargement of your hope*. Let us listen again to the silver note of the text, 'The Lord thinketh *upon me*.' The Lord thinks as much of one of his people as if there were nobody else for him to think upon. Poor needy one, ·the Lord thinks upon you as intensely as if you were the only being now existing. The Lord is able to concentrate his whole mind upon any one point without dividing that mind. He has such an infinite capacity that each one of us may be the centre of God's thoughts, and yet he will not be forgetting any other beloved one. God is a being whose centre is everywhere, but his circumference is nowhere.

Is it not beautiful to notice how God thought of the first man whom he placed on this earth? He did not make man till he had prepared everything for his happiness. The Lord would not rest until he had finished his work, until he had illuminated the heavens, and created all manner of comforts and conveniences for his child. Not till he had even prepared the birds to sing to him, and the flowers to breathe their perfume upon him, did God create man.

Why did God rest on the seventh day? Because he had thought of all that man wanted, and had made all things good for him. Our Lord Jesus never rested till he had finished the work that his Father gave him to do, which work was all for us: and the great providence of God will never rest till all the chosen of God are brought safely home to Heaven. Thus you see how God thinks upon us.

Remember also that God's thoughts are not dumb thoughts, they break out into words, and this precious Bible contains the expression of those thoughts of love. This priceless Book is a love-letter from our Father who is in Heaven. Read each line as if it were freshly written, and it will make you say, 'I am poor and needy; yet the Lord thinketh upon me, and here are his thoughts.'

God's thoughts are practical, and produce deeds of kindness; he thinks to give and forgive; to save and succour; to cheer and cherish. The Lord is thinking what he will give you, what he will make of you, and what mansion in Heaven he will appoint for you. And if he has thought upon you, he always will think upon you, for the Lord never changes. Our God, in whom we trust, is not fickle; he is not thoughtful of us today and forgetful of us tomorrow. If you should live to be as old as Methuselah, the promises of God will never wear out; and if all the troubles that ever fell upon humanity should pounce upon you, God's strength will be put forth to sustain you, and to bear you to a triumphant close. Oh, the great joy of knowing that God thinketh upon us! It is better to have God thinking upon us than to have all the kings of earth and all the angels of Heaven thinking upon us.

Thirdly, and very briefly, let this *inflame your love.* 'I am poor and needy; yet the Lord thinketh upon me.' Dear friends, think much of God, since he, by amazing grace, thinks much of you. Let your hearts go out towards *him* on whose heart your name is written. It ought to be impossible for a Christian to wander among these Menton olive groves without saying, 'Beneath such trees as these my Saviour sweated great drops of blood.' We ought not to sit near the beach without thinking, 'The Lord has cast my sins into the depths of the sea.' As the palm tree lifts itself to heaven, without an earthward branch, so send all your thoughts upward. As the vine, though sharply pruned, yields its cluster, so bear fruit unto your Lord. Upon the distant sea the apostle of the Gentiles was tossed and wrecked for love of Jesus: yield to that same Lord your whole hearts as you think upon his thoughts of you.

Everything about Menton should make us think of our Lord, for in many respects it is the counterpart of 'thy land, O Immanuel!' This day God is thinking upon you, this day think upon God. Christ in Heaven is preparing Heaven for us, let us be preparing a place on earth for him.

I have often wondered what is meant by our Lord's preparing a place for us, since Heaven is prepared for us from before the foundation of the world. I suppose Heaven was not fully fit for us till Jesus our Lord went there; and his very going has prepared Heaven for redeemed men and women to live in his own wonderful society. Our Saviour is watching in Heaven for the time when we shall come home, and he is praying for that home coming – 'Father, I will that they also, whom thou hast given me, be with me where I am.'

Do you not receive frequent tokens that the Lord Jesus is thinking upon you? Special mercies in answer to prayer, sweet visits of love; do not these cheer your heart? Our sacred joys, which come from Jesus, are like those boxes of flowers that we send to our friends who are freezing in the cold at this time in England. They know that we remember them as they look upon every rose bud, and violet, and anemone, that comes to them through the post. Our heavenly Father sends us many such tokens of his loving remembrance while we are hearing the Gospel, or enjoying the Lord's Supper, or occupied in our private prayers and meditations. 'How precious also are thy thoughts unto me, O God! how great is the sum of them!'

To close, let me use this text to *direct your conduct.* 'I am poor and needy; yet the Lord thinketh upon me.' The whole of what I say shall go into this one thought – if God thinks upon you, leave off all anxious and carking care about yourself. I do not suppose there is any place in the world that has more care and anxiety in it than this little town which nestles beneath the mountains, and suns itself by the sea. Many of you come here with dear ones who are pining away before your eyes, or you are alarmed about your own health. Do not trouble yourself unduly; for if you do so, you cannot remove sickness thereby, but you may even increase it. If I could do any good by worrying, I would worry away to my heart's content; but as it is useless, I find it best to let it alone. They tell me that if a man were to fall into the sea he would float if he remained calm, but because he struggles he sinks. I am sure it is so when we are in affliction. Fretfulness results in weakening us, in hiding from us wise methods of relief, and, in general, in doubling our pains. It is folly to kick against the pricks: it is wisdom to kiss the rod. Trust more, and fear less.

If you have trusted your soul with Christ, can you not trust him with everything else? Can you not trust him with your sick child, or your sick husband, with your wealth, with your business, with your life? 'O,' says one, 'I hardly like to do that. It is almost presumption to take our minor cares to the great Lord.' But in so doing you will prove the truthfulness of your faith!

I heard of a man who was walking along the high road, with a pack on his back: he was growing weary, and was, therefore, glad when a gentleman came along in a chaise, and asked him to take a seat with him. The gentleman noticed that he kept his pack strapped to his shoulders, and so he said, 'Why do you not put your pack down?' 'Why, sir,' said the traveller, 'I did not venture to intrude. It was very kind of you to take *me* up, and I could not expect you to carry my pack as well.'

'Why,' said his friend, 'do you not see that, whether your pack is on your back or off your back, I have to carry it?' My hearer, it is so with your trouble: whether you care, or do not care, it is the Lord who must care for you.

'But my daily trouble seems too mean a thing to bring before the Lord in prayer.' Then I fear you forget my text, or fail to see the Spirit which dictated it: God thinks upon the poor and needy, and all the concerns of the poor and needy are, like themselves, poor affairs. Why do you weary yourself with care when God cares for you? If I were afraid of burglars, and kept a watchman to guard my house at night, I certainly should not sit up all night myself. The Lord is your keeper, why are you fearful? It is infinitely better that you should be able to say, 'The Lord thinketh upon me,' than that you should have all power, and wisdom, and wealth, in your own hands. I charge you, then, to rest in the Lord, and fret no longer.

Trust your Lord with your soul, and then trust him with everything else. Surrender yourself to his love, to be saved by his infinite compassion, and then bring all your burdens, and cares, and troubles, and lay them down at his dear feet, and go and live a happy, joyful life, saying, as I will say, and close –

> *All that remains for me,*
> *Is but to love and sing;*
> *And wait until the angels come,*
> *To bear me to my King.*

A message delivered at Menton, when ill.
Edited from *The Sword and the Trowel*, May 1885.

2

The Man Whose Sword Clave to His Hand

Eleazar – A Model of Courage and
Perseverance in the Lord's Work

'And after him was Eleazar the son of Dodo the Ahohite, one of the three mighty
men with David, when they defied the Philistines that were there gathered
together to battle, and the men of Israel were gone away: he arose, and smote the
Philistines until his hand was weary, and his hand clave unto the sword: and the
Lord wrought a great victory that day' *(2 Samuel 23.9-10)*.

I N DAVID'S SERVICE we find the names of many mighty men
who came to David when his fortunes were at their lowest ebb,
and he was regarded as a rebel and an outlaw, and they remained
faithful to him throughout their lives. Weary of the evil govern-
ment of Saul, they forged a path in which they could best serve their
country and their God, and though this entailed great risks, they
were amply rewarded by the honours which in due time they shared
with their leader. When David came to the throne, how glad their
hearts must have been; and when he went on conquering, how they

must have rejoiced, each one of them remembering the privations which they had shared with their captain.

We do not aspire to be numbered with the warlike on an earthly roll of battle, but there is now being made up a roll of heroes who contend for Christ, who go outside the camp and bear his reproach. There will come a day when it will be infinitely more honourable to find one's name in the lowest place on the list of Christ's faithful disciples than to be numbered with princes and kings. Blessed are they who can this day cast in their lot with the *greater Son* of David, and share his reproach, for the day shall come when the Master's glory shall be reflected upon all his followers.

We will now turn our attention to one particular hero, Eleazar, the son of Dodo, and see what he did for his king. Our text records one of his feats. It is very instructive, and the first lesson I gather from it is *the power of individual energy*. The Philistines had started the battle and the men of Israel came out to fight them, but for some reason or other, 'being armed, and carrying bows, *[they]* turned back in the day of battle' *(Psalm 78.9)*. The record is one of initial humiliation. This man Eleazar, however, made up for the failure of his countrymen, for he 'arose, and smote the Philistines'. He was a man of marked individuality of character – a man who knew himself and knew his God, and did not care to be lost in the crowd and to run away just because they ran. He did not make the conduct of others the measure of his service, but while Israel fled he arose and smote the Philistines.

The personal obligation of each individual before God is a lesson which we should all learn. It is taught to us in our baptism, for there each believer makes his own confession of faith, and by his own act and deed acknowledges himself to be dead with Christ. Pure Christianity knows nothing of proxies or sureties in baptism. After our profession of faith is made, we are responsible for our own religious acts, and cannot employ priests or ministers to perform our religion for us; we ourselves must pray, search the Scriptures, commune with God, and obey the Lord Jesus. True religion is a personal thing. Each believer, with one talent or with ten, will on the great day of judgement be called to account for his own responsibilities, and not for those of others; and therefore he should live as before God, feeling that he is a separate individual, and must personally consecrate himself, spirit, soul, and body, entirely to the Lord.

Eleazar felt that he must do his duty whatever others might do, and therefore he drew his sword against the enemy. I do not find that he wasted time in criticising the others for running away, nor in shouting to them to return, but he just turned his own face to the enemy, and hewed and hacked away with all his might. His example was a sufficient rebuke, and far more effective than ten thousand sarcastic speeches.

Never forget that our responsibility, in a certain sense, begins and ends with ourselves. Suppose you entertain the opinion that the church of God is in a very sad state. You are responsible only as far as you yourself help to create that condition. Do you regret that many wealthy people do not consecrate their substance? The most practical thing is to use your own substance in your Master's cause. It is very easy to pick holes in other people's work, but it is far more profitable to do better yourself. Is there a fool in all the world who cannot criticise? But those who can labour well are one in a thousand compared with those who can see faults in the labours of others. Therefore, do not criticise others, but arise yourself and smite the Philistines.

Our responsibility is actually increased by the poor conduct of others. If every man fights his best, the Eleazar will do well to fight as effectively as the rest. But if others are running away, Eleazar must rise above himself and retrieve the fortunes of the day. If you are convinced that the condition of the churches is not what it should be, you must leave no stone unturned to make up the lost efficiency. Are your fellow Christians worldly? Then you should yourself become more heavenly-minded. Are they lax? You should be more strict. Are they unkind? You should be more full of love.

Perhaps Eleazar was better off for not having a cowardly crowd at his heels. When we have good work to do for our Lord we are glad of the company of kindred spirits who are determined to make the work succeed. But if we have no such comrades we must go alone. There is no absolute necessity for numbers. Poor helpers might be more of a hindrance than a help.

When Luther went to a holy man and told him what he had discovered in the Scriptures, the prudent old gentleman replied, 'My brother, go back to your cell, keep your thoughts to yourself, serve God, and make no disturbance.' But he little dreamed what disturbance Luther was about to make in the camp. I dare say Luther would not have been able to work such a reformation if he had been surrounded by such a host of prudent friends. But when he was clear of all the excellent incapables, like the hero of our text he made havoc of the Philistines of Rome. When good Christian people are for ever saying, 'Don't be too daring; be careful never to offend; don't over-exert yourself,' and all that, a believer is better off without them than with them. The Lord's servant should seek the help of his fellow believers, but, at the same time, if he is called to a service for his Lord, and they will not help him, let him not be alarmed. If he has God with him he has all the allies he needs.

Secondly, we have in the text, *a lesson of personal weakness.* Eleazar, though he arose and smote the Philistines, was only a man, and so he fought on until his hand was weary, and he could do no more. He reached the limit of his strength, and was obliged to pause. This may console those who have become exhausted in the service of God. Perhaps they blame themselves, but indeed there is no reason for doing so, for of them it may be said as of Eleazar, that they are not weary *of* fighting, though they are weary *in* fighting. If you can draw that distinction in your case it will be well.

We wish we could serve our Lord day and night, but the flesh is weak, and there is no more strength left in us. This is no strange thing, and there is no sin in it. Eleazar's weariness was that of bone, muscle and sinew. But sometimes God's people grow weary in the brain, and this is just as painful and just as little to be wondered at. The mind cannot always think with equal clearness, or feel with equal emotion, or find utterance with equal clearness, and the child of God must not blame himself for this. If a workman has been in the harvest field from the daybreak till the moon has looked down upon him as he binds his sheaves, and if, as he wipes the sweat from his brow, he says, 'Sir, I am sorely wearied, I must have a few hours' sleep,' who but a tyrant would blame him, and refuse him the rest? Those are to be blamed who never weary themselves, but those who wear themselves out are to be commended and not censured.

Perhaps Eleazar became weary because of the enormous number of his enemies. He cut dozens of them down with his sword, but on they came, and still on. Christian friend, you have been the means of bringing some few to Christ, but the appalling number of the unconverted oppresses you till your mind is weary. You have opened a little room, and a few people attend, but you say to yourself – What are these among so many? When we begin in the Master's service we think we shall turn the world upside-down in six weeks, but we do not succeed, and when we find that we must plod on and not despise the day of small things, we are apt to become weary. Lifelong service under great discouragement is not as easy as mere dreamers think.

Perhaps Eleazar grew tired because no one was helping him. It is a great assistance to receive a word of good cheer from a comrade, and to feel after all that you are not alone, for other true hearts are engaged in the same battle, zealous for the same Lord. But as Eleazar looked around, he saw only the backs of the retreating cowards, and he had to mow down the Philistines with his lone sword. Who marvels that at length he grew weary? The mercy of it all is that he became weary only when he could afford to be so. That is to say, the Lord did not allow his weariness to overcome him till he had beaten the Philistines, and the people had rushed upon the spoil. We are such very feeble things that weariness must come over us at times, but what a blessing it is that the Lord makes our strength equal to our day, and only when the day is over does he let us sink in fatigue.

Jacob wrestled with the angel, and he did not feel the shrinking sinew till he had won the blessing. It was good for him to go limping after his victory, to make him know that it was not by his own strength he had prevailed with God. And so it was a good thing for Eleazar to feel weary, for he would now understand where the strength came from with which he smote the Philistines.

Let us ask ourselves whether, weak as we are, we have given ourselves up to the Lord. If so, all is well; he will use our weakness, and glorify himself by it. He will not let our weakness show itself when it would endanger the victory. He gives us strength up to the point where strength is absolutely essential, and if he lets us collapse, as Elijah did after his great conflict was over, we must not be surprised.

What a difference there is between Elijah on Carmel triumphant over the priests of Baal, and the same man the next day fleeing from Jezebel, and crying, 'Take away my life; for I am not better than my fathers.' When we become downcast after having obtained a great blessing, do not be so terribly alarmed about it. What does it matter? The work is over; you can afford to be laid low before God. It will be good for you to know how empty and how weak you are, that you may ascribe all glory to the Lord alone.

There is a third lesson in the text, and that concerns *the intensity of the hero's zeal*. An event is here recorded – his hand clave unto his sword. Mr Bunyan seems to have thought that it was the congealed blood which fastened the hand and the sword together, for he represents Mr Valiant-for-Truth as being wounded until the blood ran forth and his hand was glued to his sword. But perhaps the better interpretation refers to a fact which has occasionally been observed in battles. I remember reading of a sailor who fought desperately in repelling a boarding attack from an enemy's ship, and when the affair was over it was found that he could not open his hand to drop his cutlass. He had grasped it with such force that until a surgical operation had been performed it was quite impossible to separate his hand from his sword. This was the case with Eleazar; this cleaving of his hand to the sword indicates the energy with which he gripped his weapon.

At first he laid hold upon it in the right way, so that he could hold it firmly. I wish that some of our converts would get hold of the Gospel in a better manner. A missionary said to me the other day, 'There are numbers of revival converts who will never be worth anything till they are converted again.' I am afraid it is so. The work is not deep. Their understanding of the Gospel is not clear. Their hold of it is not fast. They have got something which is of great good to them, I hope, but they hardly know what it is; they need to come again to him who has abundance of grace and Truth to bestow, or they will never be worth much. Many young people do not study the Word seriously. They pick up texts here and there as pigeons pick up peas, and they do not see the whole faith. The person destined to fight for God lays hold of Truth by the handle and grips it as one who knows what he has. He who intelligently and intensely knows the Word is likely to hold it fast.

Eleazar, having grasped his sword well, retained his hold; whatever happened to him in battle, he never let go of his weapon for an instant. If he had once opened his hand there would have been no cleaving, but all the way through he kept his hand on his weapon. I have frequently been moved to observe the perseverance of earnest workers, who have loved their work for Christ so strongly that they could not cease from it. They have served the Lord year after year in a particular work, either in the Sunday School or in some other labour, and when they have been ill and could no longer be in their place, their hearts and their thoughts have still been there. I have known them when feverish, talking continually about the Schools and the children. Even in their dreams their good work has been on their minds. Their hand has cleaved to the sword.

I delight to hear the elderly talk about the work of the Lord even when they can no longer join in it, and the dying, with 'the ruling passion strong in death', enquiring about the church and the services, their swords cleaving still to their hands. Christmas Evans used to drive his old pony from town to town on his journeys to preach the Gospel, and when he came near to die he thought he was riding in the old pony-chaise still, and his last words were, 'Drive on!'

Years ago we who believed grasped the Lord with such a grip of cheerful earnestness that now there is established an almost involuntary connection with him which cannot be severed. Every now and then some wise people think to convert us to scepticism or 'modern thought', and they try to get us to give up our old-fashioned faith. They are fools for their pains, for we are now hardly voluntary agents in the matter: the Gospel has such a hold upon us that we cannot let it go. We now believe because we must. I would sooner die a thousand deaths than renounce the Gospel I preach.

The arguments I have met with in sceptical books are not half so strong as the arguments with which the devil has assailed me, and yet I have beaten him. How can we give up the Gospel? It is our life, our soul, our all. Our daily experience, our communion with God, our sitting with Christ in heavenly places, have all made us resistant to every temptation to give up our hope. We hold our sword, it is true, but our sword also cleaves to our hand. It is not possible that the most clever falsehoods should deceive the elect, for the Lord has created such communion between the renewed soul and the Truth, that the Truth must hold us, and we must hold the Truth, even till we die. God grant it may be so with all of you.

I must pass on to the fourth lesson – and that concerns *the divine glory*. Does the text say that his hand clave unto the sword, and that *he* wrought a great victory that day? It does not ascribe the victory to Eleazar, but it is written, 'And *the Lord* wrought a great victory that day.' The victory was not won without Eleazar, and yet it was not by Eleazar, but by the Lord. Had Eleazar belonged to a certain spiritual viewpoint he would have said, 'We can do nothing; the Lord will fulfil his own eternal purposes;' and then he would not only have done nothing, but he would have found fault with others if they had been forward in the fight. If he had belonged to another group of Christians he would have said, 'I do not believe in the one-man ministry. I will not go alone, but wait till I have gathered a few brethren, who can all take a turn at it.' Instead of either of these theorisings he went straight to his work, and the Lord gave him the necks of his enemies, and then he ascribed the victory, not to himself but to the Lord alone.

The right thing to do is to work as if all depended upon us, and yet look to the Lord alone, knowing that all depends upon him. We must have all the humility and all the activity of those who feel that they cannot do anything by themselves but that God works in them to will and to do, according to his own good pleasure.

You must be humbly reliant on God, and personally resolute. Have you won a soul to Christ? Then the Lord has won the victory. Have you upheld the Truth against an antagonist? The Lord must have the glory of your triumph. Have you trampled down sin? Can you cry with the heroine of old, 'O my soul, thou hast trodden down strength'? Lay your trophies at the foot of the throne. I am glad that my text runs as it does, or else some critic would have said that I was exalting man, and honouring flesh and blood. The Lord has wrought all our works in us: not unto us, but unto his name give praise.

The last lesson is one of *encouragement.* It is said in the text that 'the people returned after him only to spoil.' Does it grieve you to think that many professing Christians seem more like unbelievers than believers? Do you feel sad to see them all run away in the day of battle? Be comforted, then, for they can be brought back, and your personal prowess for God may be the means of making them return. The feeble folk, if the Lord makes *you* strong, will gather courage from your bravery. They may not have been able to look a live Philistine in the face, but they know how to strip a dead one. You will get them back by and by, when the spoil is to be divided.

It has sometimes happened that one man, speaking in God's name, has turned a community in the right way: one Christian woman, too, has swayed thousands. There are points in the history of England where certain individuals have been the hinge upon which our nation's destiny has turned.

If you seek to be faithful, then be firm in the day of battle, and you will confirm wavering souls. My young sister, you will turn your family round yet: one by one they will come to seek your Saviour. Young man, you are entering into that large business; it is very perilous to you, but, if the Lord enables you to be strong in the power of his might, you may transform that firm into a church of God. You may hardly believe it, but you may yet have prayer meetings in a large room somewhere in that firm. Many cowards are skulking about – try to shame them. Many are undecided, let them see a brave believer, and he will be the standard-bearer around whom they will rally.

It is clear that when a man gets hold of a sword, grips it fast, and holds it for a while, such a thing may happen that he cannot drop it. Has it ever occurred to us that if we eagerly hold on to sin, it may produce a similar result? One of these days we may be unable to get rid of those habits which we are now forming. At first the net of habit is made of cobweb – you can easily break through it. By and by, it is made of twine; soon it will be made of rope; and last of all it will be as strong as steel, and then you will be fatally ensnared. Beware in time!

Young people, you are hardly yet aware how strong a hold your habits have already taken on you. I mean your habits of prayerlessness, your practice of secret sin, and your lack of self-control. They are fastening on you like huge serpents, coil upon coil. You have always intended to go so far and no further, but if you could see a picture of what you will become, you would be horrified. We read in the papers a few months ago the story of a man who was respectable in many ways, and gifted above the average of men, who nevertheless descended by degrees till he committed a horrible crime which made the world aghast. Little did he dream at one time that he would have plunged into such wickedness. But the path to hell is downhill, and if you descend one step at first, you take two steps at once next time, and then you take four, and so by great leaps descend to hell. Throw away the weapon of iniquity before it glues itself to your hand. Cast it away once and for ever.

The only way of breaking with sin is to unite with Christ. 'If the Son therefore shall make you free, ye shall be free indeed.' Seek that freedom. May he bestow it upon every one of us, and then may we become heroes of Christ, and he shall have the glory, for ever and ever.

Edited from a prayer-meeting address in *The Sword and the Trowel*, October 1876

3

Inspiration for Seekers and Veteran Believers
Following the Father's Will

'Jesus saith unto them, My meat is to do the will of him that sent me, and to finish his work' *(John 4.34)*.

THIS TEXT CONTAINS much consolation for those who search for salvation, and provides a supreme example to those who are saved. Let us begin by noticing that the text contains much encouragement for seekers. Those burdened by a sense of sin will note that the work of saving souls is called by Christ – his Father's will. There is a tendency to imagine that Christ is full of pity, but the Father is austere, severe, and an avenging judge. The Saviour, however, says that the work of mercy is 'the will of him that sent me'. In other words, he effectively says, 'All that I am doing when I seek the soul of a poor, sinful, Samaritan woman by this well, is in agreement with my Father's mind.' Christ was bringing to reconciliation with God those whom the benevolent will of the Father said should be saved.

Seeker, if you find yourself in the garden of the household of God you have not come here as an intruder, for the gate is open and it is God's will that you should come. If you receive Christ into your heart, you will not have stolen the treasure; it was God's will that you should receive Christ. If with broken heart you come and rest on the finished sacrifice of Jesus, you need not fear that you will violate the eternal purpose, or come into collision with the divine decree, for God's will has brought you into this condition. One of the most groundless fears a person can entertain is the dread that the Father will be unwilling to forgive. If *you* desire, *God* has long ago desired. If *you* determine in your heart to find God, *he* has long ago determined it. You need never be troubled about divine predestination.

Rest assured that God has never spoken in secret, in some dark place of the earth, and said, 'Seek my face in vain.' He has never passed a secret decree in the eternal council chamber which shall contravene the open promise of his mercy – whosoever believeth on the Son hath everlasting life. If you come to Christ and cast yourself upon him, you need entertain no fear that you are violating the will of God, for salvation is the will of God which Jesus Christ has come to fulfil.

Another consolation is given here to every seeking soul, namely, that *Jesus Christ is sent into the world on purpose to save.* If I know that I am sick, and that a physician has come for the express purpose of healing, I feel no difficulty about inviting him into my house. If I know that I am poor, and that a rich benefactor has come with the express intention of liberally helping the poor, I have no difficulty in approaching him.

Similarly, wherever there is an empty sinner, a full Christ has come for the purpose of filling that empty sinner. If you hunger after Christ, rest assured that Christ has met with you, and sees you as one of those whom he came to call. He would not have made you hunger, nor made you thirst, nor made you feel your emptiness, if it had not been his intention to remove that hunger, slake that thirst, and fill that emptiness to the full. Never indulge the thought that he came to save better ones than you, and that you are beyond the pale of his mercy, but instead let your sinfulness, nothingness, conscious weakness and condemnation inspire you with a surer hope that you are the very person Jesus Christ came to deliver. He came to seek and to save that which was lost. Who is more lost than you? Here, then, is a double comfort: it is both the will of God and the mission of Christ that sinners should be saved.

Perhaps the greatest encouragement to a despairing sinner in this text is *the delight which Jesus Christ experiences in the work of saving souls.* This was his one object. From eternity past he looked forward to the day when a body should be prepared for him so that he might come into the world to redeem the lost. Then, when the fulness of time was come, he was no unwilling servant to our souls. 'In the volume of the book it is written of me, I delight to do thy will, O my God.' Down from the portals of the skies the Saviour came with glad alacrity, willing to save. When he was on earth he was never reluctant to seek out the guilty. He could have healed the leper, if he had wanted, while standing at a distance, but he chose to touch him when he healed him, to show that he did not shrink from helping humanity. This was his delight.

He did not surround himself with a bodyguard to keep off the throng, but was among them, often surrounded by a multitude of common folk. He put himself at the beck and call of everyone. He had not time so much as to eat, and when he did seek a little rest, they followed him on foot and pressed him with their entreaties. He was never angry, but always full of compassion towards them. Christ was a willing Saviour, and found his soul's delight in winning souls. Even the great crowning work of suffering and death by which souls were redeemed was no unwilling service. He said he had a baptism to be baptised with, and that he was straitened until it was accomplished. The cup was bitter as hell, but he longed to drink it.

His death was to be at once the most ignominious and the most painful that could be devised, and yet he thirsted for it. 'With desire I have desired to eat this passover,' he said. He did not hide himself away when he was sought by his murderers, but went to the garden. Judas knew the place, and when they sought him he said, 'Are ye come out, as against a thief, with swords and with staves?' He was willing to yield himself up. No bonds could have bound him, and yet he offered himself. They could not have dragged him to the cross, nor myriads like them, but he went like 'a lamb to the slaughter, and as a sheep before her shearers is dumb, so he openeth not his mouth'. All that wondrous passion upon Calvary was a free-will, voluntary sacrifice to the fullest possible degree. I may even say that in his deepest agony Christ had a joy unknown. I think we have too much forgotten the wonderful joy which must have filled the Saviour's heart even when going to the cross.

Dear friends, if you have a benevolent nature, you cannot suffer for others without feeling joy that you are taking the suffering from them. We know that it was because of 'the joy that was set before him' that he 'endured the cross, despising the shame'. As the Lord dived into the black waves of grief he could see the precious pearl which he counted to be of greater price than all, and that sight sustained him with a latent joy. This joy may not have appeared to onlookers at the time, but it lay slumbering within his soul even when he was 'exceeding sorrowful, even unto death'.

Now that he has gone up on high, he has no greater joy than this – in seeing souls redeemed by him. Jesus wept over Jerusalem because it would not be saved, but he rejoices greatly over sinners who repent. This is his happiness, and his crown of rejoicing – even poor fearful seekers who come and look to him and find their healing in his wounds.

I would urge those of you who desire to find peace and faith, to make a point of thinking very much about Christ. We not only lay hold on the cross by faith, but it is the cross which works faith in us. If you would think more often of the mercy of God, and the will of

God, and the mission of Christ, and the lovingkindness of Christ, your soul would probably be led by the Spirit, through that course of thought, to believe in him. Dwelling constantly upon your sin and your hardness of heart tends to drive you to despair.

It is well to know that your heart is hard, and your sin great, but a person is not healed simply by knowing that he is sick, nor will he get comfort by merely studying his disease. So you are not likely to find faith by raking amongst the baseness of your fallen nature, or trying to find something good in yourself which is not there. Your wisest course is to think much of Christ, and look to him. You will soon find hope in him if you look for it in him. You will soon discover grounds for comfort if you look to God in the person of his Son.

If you consider the will of God as it is revealed on Calvary, and read it in the crimson lines written on the Saviour's pierced body, you will soon perceive that his will is love. Look away from your own state of death, to the death of Jesus. I urge you to receive the truth which I have put before you, and which the text so plainly presents. The salvation of sinners is the will of God, the work of Christ, and the joy of Christ. Is not this good news?

But I said that the text was also an example to believers, and so it is. The more we become like him, the more we attain to what God would have us be. Note in the text, first of all, Christ's *subservience*. He says, 'My meat is to do the will of him that sent me.' He says nothing about his own will. Did he not say, 'Not my will, but thine, be done'? The person of the world thinks that if he could have his own way he would be perfectly happy, and his dream of happiness is comprised in this, that his own wishes will be gratified, his own longings fulfilled, his own desires granted to him. This is all a mistake. A person will never be happy in this way. Perfect happiness is to be found in exactly the opposite direction, namely, in the casting down of our own will entirely, and asking that the will of God may be fulfilled in us.

'This is my meat,' says the sinner, 'to do my own will.' Jesus Christ points to another table, and says, 'This is my meat, to do the will of him that sent me. My greatest comfort, and the most substantial nourishment of my spirit, are not found in carrying out my own desires, but in submitting all my desires to the will of the Father.' Beloved, our sorrows grow from the roots of our self-will. Would we have deep sorrow if we were really submitted to the will of God? Pain would have a wonderful sweetness, losses would become things to rejoice in, and we would even take joyfully the destruction of our goods.

Another matter to notice in this text is something other than subservience. It is a *recognised commission*. Let it be our desire also to see clearly our commission from on high. Christ speaks of '*the will of him that sent me*'. If I am a soldier sent on a mission, I do not have to consider *what* I shall do, for having received my commands I am bound to obey. Do not many Christians fail to see their commission?

It has come to be a dreadfully common belief in the Christian church that the only person who has a 'call' is the one who devotes all his time to the 'ministry', whereas all Christian service is ministry, and every Christian has a call to some kind of ministry or another. It is not every person who can become an instructor or an exhorter, but each one must minister according to the gift received. We are a nation of priests. As believers we are sent into this world with a distinct commission, and that is very like the commission given to our Master. In our measure the Spirit of the Lord is upon us, to bind up the broken-hearted, to proclaim liberty to the captives, and to preach the acceptable year of the Lord.

The work of atonement we cannot share, for Christ has trodden the winepress alone, but the place of service is our dwelling-place. Christ's dying commission, not to the apostles only, but to all the saints, is this: 'As my Father hath sent me, even so send I you.' When Christ was sent of God he did not forget that he was sent. He did not come into this world to do his own business. So you and I must not act as though we were here just to make money or bring up our families, and make matters comfortable for ourselves. We are sent into the world on a divine errand, and we need grace to recognise the errand and to perform it.

Further, notice *the practical character of our Lord's observations on these two points.* He says, 'My meat is' – what? To consider? To resolve? To calculate? To study prophecy as to when the world will end? To meditate upon plans by which we may be able one of these days to do something great? Not at all. 'My meat is to do the will of him that sent me.' The meat of some people is to find fault with others who do Christ's will. They never seem to have their mouths so well filled as when remarking upon the imperfections of those who are vastly better than themselves. Did you ever know a man whom God blessed who had not some crotchet or singularity? Whenever God blesses us there is sure to be something or other to remind others that the vessel containing the treasure is an earthen vessel. Were critics wise they would understand that this is a part of the divine appointment, that we should have this treasure in earthen vessels, that the excellency of the power may be of God, and not of us.

There are others, of a somewhat better disposition, who find their meat in projecting new methods, and who invent grand schemes. They are always talking of some great scheme or other for impossible Christian union, or some magnificent but impracticable Christian effort. Our Lord was practical. You are struck throughout his life with the practical character of it. He was no visionary, and no fanatic. Though his holy soul was on fire, all his plans and methods were the wisest that could possibly be arranged. I hope we shall be the same.

Some Christians are too fond of mysticisms, quibbles, oddities, and strange questions which minister not unto profit. I heartily wish they would try to win souls for Christ in the old-fashioned biblical way. Every now and then some particular phase of truth crops up, and certain Christians go perfectly mad about it, wanting to pry between leaves that are folded, or to find out secrets which are not revealed, or to reach some fancied eminence of self-conceited perfection in the flesh. While there are so many sinners to be lost or to be saved, I believe we had better keep to preaching the Gospel. As long as this world contains millions of those who do not know even the elementary truths of Christianity, would it not be the best priority for us to go into the highways and hedges, and tell men of our dying Saviour, and point them to the cross? Let us discuss the millennium, and the secret rapture, and all those other intricate questions by-and-by, when we have got through more pressing needs.

Just now the vessel is going to pieces; who will man the lifeboat? The house is ablaze, and who will run the fire-escape up to the window? Here are men perishing for lack of knowledge, and who will tell them that there is life in a look at the crucified One? Christ's satisfaction of heart was of a most practical kind; he was subservient to God as a commissioned servant; and he was busy actually *doing* the will of God.

For all that we have said, the gist of our text lies here: that our *Lord Jesus Christ found both sustenance and delight in the will of God in the winning of souls.* Read the diaries of Whitefield and of Wesley and you will be struck with the fact that you do not find them perpetually doubting their calling, mistrusting their election, or questioning whether they love the Lord or not. Visualise them preaching to thousands in the open air, and hearing around them cries of 'What must we do to be saved?' and you will see that they had no time for doubts and fears. Their full hearts had no room for such lumber. Such evangelists felt that God had sent them into this world to win souls for Christ, and they could not afford to live desponding, mistrustful lives. They lived unto God, and the Holy Ghost lived so mightily in them that they were fully assured of his marvellous power.

Some believers who do nothing except read 'Plymouthy' books, go to Bible readings and prophetic conferences, and other forms of spiritual dissipation, would be far better Christians if they would just roll up their sleeves for work, and go and tell the Gospel to dying people. All feeding and no working makes men spiritual dyspeptics. Be idle, with nothing to live for, nothing to care for, no sinner to pray for, no backslider to lead back to the cross, no trembler to encourage, no little child to tell of a Saviour, no object, in fact, to live for; and who wonders, if you begin to groan and murmur and look within. But if the Master shall come to you, and put his hand upon you, and say – 'I have sent you just as my Father sent me; now go and do my will,' you will find that in keeping his commandments there is great reward.

Let us have practical Christianity, my brethren. Let us never neglect doctrinal Christianity, nor experimental Christianity, but if we do not have the practice of it in being to others what Christ was to us, we shall soon find the experience to be flavoured with bitterness. Christ found joy in seeking the good of the Samaritan woman. Her heart, hitherto unrenewed, satisfied him when he had won it to himself.

But, notice, our Lord says in addition to his finding it his meat to do God's will, that he also *desired to finish* his work. And this is our soul's satisfaction, to persevere until our work is finished. We do not know how near we may be to the completion of our work. The chariot-wheels of eternity sound behind us. Let us use the moments zealously, for they are very precious. 'I paint for eternity,' said the painter. So let us work for God as those whose fruit will endure when all burns in the last tremendous fire.

When David Brainerd the great missionary to the Indians was dying, the last thing he did was to teach a little child its letters, and when someone marvelled to see so great a man at such a work, he said he thanked God that when he could no longer preach he had enough strength left to teach that poor little child. So would he finish his life's work, and put in the last little stroke to complete the picture. It should be our meat and our drink to push on, never finding our meat in what we have done, but in what we are doing and still have to do; always finding our refreshment in the work of the present hour as God enables us to perform it.

Let us never say, 'I have had my day; let the young people take their turn.' Imagine the stars in their beauty saying, 'We have for so long a time shot our golden arrows through the darkness, we will now retire for ever.' What if the air should refuse to give us breath, or the water should no longer ripple in its channels, or if all nature should stand still because of what it once did? What death and ruin there would be. No, Christian, there must be no loitering for you. Every day may this be your meat – to do the will of him that sent you, and to finish his work.

Finally, a word of reflection on the glory which Jesus Christ should have from us. How could he ever have loved us? It is strange that the Son of God should have set his affections upon such unworthy beings. It is the wonder of all wonders that he should have come to save us; when we were so lost and ruined that we did not even care about his love, rejected it when we heard of it, and despised it even as it came with power to our hearts.

Yet he has no greater delight than in saving us, and in bringing us to glory. Do not our hearts say within us, 'O! what shall I do, my Saviour, to praise? How shall I show forth my gratitude to him who found such delight in serving me?' From this day forth may it be our meat and drink to do the will of him that sent us, and to finish his work. I leave the text with you, my hearers in Christ, and may God give you grace to translate its meaning into practical action. I leave the text also with those who are unconverted, and may it be as cords of love to draw you to Christ, and the praise shall be his for ever and ever.

A brief talk from *The Sword and the Trowel,* 1873

4
Extraordinary Thought-Reading
The Basis of True Prayer

'Lord, thou hast heard the desire of the humble: thou wilt prepare their heart, thou wilt cause thine ear to hear' *(Psalm 10.17)*.

I T IS NOT A VAIN THING to wait upon God; it is your comfort, your strength, your life. Any person admitted to audience with the Most High is honoured to an unspeakable degree. The lowliest form of prayer may be most true and acceptable, and this lowliest form of prayer is described in the text – 'The desire of the humble'. It is not the prayer of the serene faith of Abraham, nor the wrestling of energetic Jacob, nor the intercession of prevailing Moses, nor the pleading of holy Samuel, nor the commanding cry of Elias shutting and opening Heaven: it is only a desire – a motion of the heart towards good things – and yet the Lord hears it.

This lowliest form of prayer may be the truest; for the essence of all real prayer is desire. Words are but the 'house' of prayer, the living tenant is desire. Other forms of prayer may be attractive to man, and yet they may have no influence whatever with the living God; but this manner of supplication has been successful from of old, as it is written – 'He will fulfil the desire of them that fear him,' and again, 'The desire of the righteous shall be granted.' In fact, prayer is desire, as our poet puts it:

> Prayer is the soul's sincere desire,
> Uttered or unexpressed;
> The motion of a hidden fire,
> That trembles in the breast.

Notice, this kind of prayer is only *a desire*. A desire may be unattended by speech. The supplicant may not be able to put his desire into words at all, for he may be too sorrowful, or his emotion may choke his utterance. He may be only able to pour forth groanings that cannot be uttered, and tears whose eloquence is silent, yet God is pleased to hear the desire which lacks expression. Many prayers are very prettily expressed; in fact, they are expressed so grandly that their fineries will not be tolerated in Heaven. Prayers will never enter Heaven's gate which are meant to catch the applause of man. God will say, 'They were meant for men, and let men have them.' He does not stoop to accept man's leftovers, and if a prayer is meant to be a feast for man, God will not be a second-rate guest at its table.

A believer may have a wealth of desire and a poverty of everything else, and yet he may be heard of the Lord. Possibly his confession may run thus – 'I desire to be humble, but I lament my pride; I desire to be strong in faith, but I mourn my unbelief; I desire to be fervent, but I sigh over my lukewarmness; I desire to be holy, but I confess my transgressions.' If your heart seethes and boils with desires, the steam thereof will rise to Heaven. Your desires have voices of their own: they knock hard at Heaven's door, and it shall be opened unto them.

Note that your desire may not even be accompanied by any confident expectation. When you pray you ought to believe the promise and expect its fulfilment, for it is the duty of every supplicant to believe that when he prays in the name of Jesus he will be heard. But sometimes humility, which is a good thing, is attended by a lack of faith, which is an evil thing; and this much hinders prayer. Humility is deceived by unbelief, and so it gives way to the dark thought that its poor feeble prayer will not have a ready hearing. I fear that in some cases this lack of expectancy is an effectual barrier to prayer, and prevents it being answered; but it is forgiven to naturally despondent, heavily-laden spirits, whose fears are not so much doubts of God as a deeply humiliating judgement of themselves. It is not so much the case that their faith is sinfully defective as that they have a painfully acute sense of their own unworthiness, and so when they cry they *hope* that the Lord will hear them, and they mean to wait upon him till he does; but they are afraid. They will go nowhere else, for their only hope lies in the free grace and sovereign mercy of God, but yet they do not exercise happy expectation.

My brethren, I would chide your unbelief, but I would still encourage your desires, for the text says, 'Lord, thou hast heard the desire of the humble.' The Lord will yet hear your humble sighs, and you will be surprised to find the Lord doing for you exceeding abundantly above what you asked or even thought. May your faith grow exceedingly.

This leads me to observe that this form of prayer which the Lord hears is described as 'the desire of the humble'. It has this advantage about it, that it is free from pride. Do not be startled to hear me say – I fear that many people ask to be humble in order that they may be admired for it. Some seek great grace so that they may be highly thought of in the market of the church. Have we not all found that in the rushing stream of our earnest zeal there will be some back-current which runs not towards God but towards ourselves? Have we not even striven to win souls so that we might be notable as soul-winners? 'Come with me, and see my zeal for the Lord,' has been the language of many a Jehu. It is hard to keep out pride.

This psalm says much concerning the proud man and the

oppressor, whom God abhors, and will surely visit in judgement; and then shines forth this bright word, like a lone star in a dark night. Never was precious pearl found in a rougher oyster shell. May the Lord keep us humble if we are so, and make us humble if we are not so.

I believe every Christian has a choice between being humble and being humbled. Now, to be humble is a sweet thing; there is no lovelier spot on the road to the Celestial City than the Valley of Humiliation. He that lives in it dwells among flowers and birds, and may sing all day long, like the shepherd boy whose song ran thus –

> He that is down need fear no fall,
>   He that is low no pride;
> He that is humble ever shall
>   Have God to be his guide.

If you do not choose to be humble you will have to be humbled; and that is not at all a desirable thing. To be humbled is to be sorely smitten and made to suffer shame in the estimation of your fellow men, both ungodly and godly. Certain persons who have carried their heads very high have struck them against the beam, and have had to go with bruised foreheads for the rest of their lives. God resisteth the proud, but giveth grace to the humble. Therefore may God help us to offer before him 'the desire of the humble'.

If you would be heard in prayer you must come to God as needy and empty. Low thoughts of ourselves are the companions of prevailing prayer. No person may expect to receive out of the fulness that is treasured up in Christ Jesus until he is willing to confess his own poverty. Grace for grace will be given only to those who feel need upon need; all successful pleadings must find their argument in free grace. We must never urge claims against the Lord as though he were our debtor; for then mercy will not deal with us. We will have appealed unto the Caesar of justice and unto Caesar we must go. Let us have done with merits and deserts, and let this be our cry, 'For thy mercy and for thy truth's sake, and for thy Son's sake, hear thou the voice of my prayer.' This is the proper Gospel spirit; and if we plead in any other fashion we shall be sent empty away.

Our second point is that *God is quick to hear the lowliest prayer.* We have heard a good deal about thought-reading. I give no opinion of that matter among men; but here is a wonderful instance of it with the Lord. 'Thou hast heard the desire of the humble.' This kind of desire-reading is the prerogative of God alone. He knows our desires even when we do not know them ourselves. Sitting in this Tabernacle you are desiring, but it is quite impossible for the person sitting next to you to know your wishes, and it is just as well perhaps. The Lord is reading your thoughts now. Your groaning out of the very deeps ascends to the heights. You would not like to tell your inward feelings: perhaps your secret is too painful to be told. But God's hearing is so acute that he can hear your desires. Wonderful art! We should be very glad if the Lord had promised to hear us when we speak; but he has gone far beyond that, and he hears the unspeakable and unutterable. Was there ever power and pity like this?

Thirdly, we will remark that *the heart is the main matter in prayer.* Desires are the fruit of the heart. The heart is the source, the seat, and the essence of supplication. Prayer with the heart is the heart of prayer. Without the heart prayer is a wretched mockery. There is as much grace in the bark of a dog or the grunt of a swine as in a form of prayer if the heart be absent. God is as likely to hear the cry of ravens than to regard prayers uttered in chapels or churches, if the mind is not in earnest.

I fear that much so-called public prayer is nothing better than presumptuous sin. If your child should come to you and ask a favour in an affected voice, would you notice him? If, instead of saying, 'Dear father, I want so-and-so,' he should take up a book and intone such words as these, 'Dearly beloved father, I have to request of thee that thou in thy great affection wilt give unto me such and such things,' you would not regard his nonsense. You would say, 'Come, boy, what do you want? Tell me plainly.' I fear that praying in sing-song is the most fearful mockery God ever hears. Imagine Peter, when he was beginning to sink, intoning, 'Lord, save me.' When the heart really gets to speak with God, it cannot talk in affected tones: it throws such rubbish overboard.

But cannot a man pray with his heart and yet use a written prayer? Certainly he can. Many have done so for years. If you cannot walk without your crutches, I would sooner you walked with them than not at all. Still it is not the best words put together by the most devout men that ever lived, nor the holiest language composed extemporaneously by yourself, that can make up prayer if the heart be gone. Words are seldom more than the baggage of prayer. Language at best is but the flesh in which prayer is embodied: the desire of the heart is the life of the prayer.

He that prays with little desire asks God to refuse him. If you go through your prayer, and your mind is wandering up and down among a thousand vanities, your desires are feeble, and your supplication will have little effect. Prayer must be fervent to be effectual; it must be ardent to be acceptable. If the utter failure of your prayer would not grieve you, and if its success would not much gratify you, then depend upon it you will have to wait long at mercy's wicket gate to be admitted.

Importunity is indispensable: our Lord has given us many parables to that effect. To play at praying will never do: heart and soul must be fully awake; for no sleepy prayer can enter Heaven. We must praise God with our whole heart, and we must pray in the same manner. If a double-minded man may not expect to receive anything of the Lord, neither may a half-hearted man. When the soul grows warm, the spirit fervent, and desires are strong, then do not spare your prayers. We are not always in that condition, so let us pray much when we are. We are bound to prepare ourselves for prayer; but I believe the best qualifications are strong desires and intense longings. No preparation for food is equal to intense hunger.

It will be your wisdom when your desires are acute to pray more than you ordinarily do. You cannot always pray like this, but when good times come use them. When a fair wind fills the sails of desire, then make all possible headway. Set apart a longer season for private devotion when the soul is all alive. At another time you may have to try very hard and make but small progress, let it not at such a time be a source of regret that you wasted a happier season. Cease not to obtain blessings beyond number both for yourself, for the church, and for a perishing world; but take heed that your heart be greatly exercised with longings for souls before God.

The Lord prepares his people's hearts by giving them a deep sense of what they need. You have grief, temptation, and hardship, and your spirit cries out under the lashes of conscience; but all this is right, because by this means you are instructed in the art and mystery of supplication. Nobody cries to Christ so well as the man who is beginning to sink. Jonah's cry in the whale's belly was the most intense prayer he ever prayed. When your spirit is overwhelmed with sorrow, then look up to Christ, the Saviour, and find him to your soul's joy. Our desires are apt to sleep, but when the Lord by his Spirit reveals to us our spiritual poverty, we long, and pine, and sigh for spiritual blessings.

Give your heart up to the Holy Spirit that he may prepare you to seek the blessing, and prepare you to receive the blessing when the time comes for the Lord to grant it. This is wonderful condescension on God's part, and on our part we ought to feel the utmost encouragement to prepare our own hearts for earnest supplication. Where God leads you to pray he means you to receive. You find a holy desire in your heart; the Lord put that desire into your heart, and for the honour of his infinite majesty, lest he stain his goodness and dishonour his great name, he must hear you.

With such comfort would I address those here who are just beginning to pray. I know I speak to some who tell us you are seeking peace, and that day and night the desire for salvation occupies the entire chamber of your soul. Well, this did not come from your own nature. Neither devil nor the old nature has taught you to pray like this. Dear hearer, be sure that the great Father who is moving you to cry to him, is hearing you, and will incline his ear to catch the faintest appeal of your spirit. Believe that he is hearing you, and cast yourself at the feet of his dear Son. Behold the wounds of Jesus, and let these invite you to draw nigh to God. I know of no more eloquent words than the wounds of the dying Lord. Let them persuade you to come to him and to trust and rest at his feet, for since he has inclined your heart to pray, he is surely about to hear you and bless you.

Edited from a sermon preached at the
Metropolitan Tabernacle, October 5th 1884

5

Sweet Fruit from a Thorny Tree
The Purposes of Pain

'We know that all things work together for good to them that love God'
(Romans 8.28).

A T TIMES WHEN our heavenly Father weighs out to us a portion of wormwood and gall in the form of bodily pain, we very naturally ask the reason why. Human nature at times asks the question in petulance, and gets no answer. Faith asks with bated breath and gains a gracious reply. Our Lord has a right to do with us as he wills, and his dispensations are not to be challenged as though he were bound to give an account of his doings at the bar of our bewildered reason. Still, if we are fully persuaded that the Lord always acts in love and wisdom, we may enquire into his design, and so far as experience can help, we may see the result of the suffering which he inflicts.

What are the comfortable fruits of righteousness which are produced by watering the soul from the bitter lakes? What are the jewels of silver and gold with which we are adorned when we leave the Egyptian bondage of pain and weariness? May I, who have of late been a prisoner of the Lord in the sick chamber, witness my confession.

1 To reduce our self-esteem

First, *pain teaches us our nothingness*. Health permits us to swell in self-esteem, and gather much which is unreal, whereas sickness makes our feebleness conspicuous, and at the same time breaks up many of our shams. We need solid grace when we are thrown into the furnace of affliction: gilt and tinsel shrivel up in the fire. The *patience* in which we rather prided ourselves – where is it when sharp pangs succeed each other like poisoned arrows setting the blood on fire? The joyful faith which could do all things and bear all sufferings, is it always at hand when the time of trial arrives? The peace which stood aloft on the mountain's summit and serenely smiled on storms beneath, does it hold its ground quite so easily as we expected when the day of battle comes?

How have I felt dwarfed and diminished by pain and depression! The preacher to thousands could creep into a nutshell, and feel himself smaller than the worm which bored the tiny round hole by which he entered. I have admired and envied the least of my Lord's servants, and desired their prayers for me, though I felt unworthy of the kind thoughts of the weakest of them.

We are most of us far too great. A soap bubble has a scant measure of material in it for its size, and most of us are after the same order. It is greatly for our good to be reduced to our true dimensions. In stormy weather a low bush or narrow eaves may shelter a sparrow, while a larger bird must bear the beat of the rain and the wind. To be nothing, and to feel less than nothing, is most sweet, for then we cower down under the great wings of God as the little chick beneath the brooding hen, and in utter helplessness we find our strength and solace.

Nothing is lost, except that which ought to go: the flower falls, but the seed ripens. When nothing remains but the clinging of a weeping child who grasps his Father's hand, nothing but the last resolve, 'Though he slay me, yet will I trust in him,' no real loss has been sustained. Rather, a great gain has come to the humbled heart.

2 To isolate us from burdens

Secondly, *heavy sickness and crushing pain isolate us from a thousand minor cares.* During such a season we cannot be cumbered with much serving, for others must take our place and be Martha in our stead. It is good if we are then enabled to take Mary's place and even lie at Jesus' feet. With me it has been so. I could do nothing for that beloved congregation and church. I have been forced to leave them with the great Shepherd and with those dear associates whom he has called to share my burden. Those orphans, how could I watch over them? Those students, how could I instruct them? Those colporteurs, how could I provide for them? What if funds run low? They must do so. I could not increase the flow of the brook Cherith, nor even find out a widow of Zarephath whose barrel of meal and cruse of oil should never waste.

The Lord must do all, or it must remain undone. The weary head could only exaggerate the need, and the sinking spirits could not suggest a supply. All must be left; yes, *must* be left. The reins drop from the driver's hands; the ploughman forgets the furrow; the seed-basket hangs no longer on the sower's arm. Thus is the soul shut in with God as within a wall of fire, and all her thought must be of him, and of his promise and his help. We are forced to lie as one dead at the feet of the great Lord, and look up and hope.

This cutting loose from earthly shores, this rehearsal of what must soon be done once for all in the hour of departure, is a salutary exercise, tending to cut away the hampering encumbrances of this mortal life, and make us free for the heavenly race. It is well to have those windows which look towards earth and its cares closed, that we may be driven to that fairer prospect which lies on the other side of Jordan. This is not the natural effect of pain, but when the Spirit of God works by it, the help that way is wonderful.

3 To increase our fervour

Thirdly, *sickness has caused many workers to become more intense when they have again been favoured to return to their place.* We lie and bemoan our shortcomings, discovering faults which in healthier hours had escaped notice, resolving, in God's strength, to throw our energies more fully into the weightiest matters and spend less of force on secondary things. How much lasting good shall come of this! The time, apparently wasted, may turn out for a more efficient use of life if the worker shall be more earnest, more careful, more prayerful, more dependent upon God, and more passionately set upon doing his Lord's business thoroughly, for years to come.

O that we could all thus utilise our seasons of sickness! Then should we come forth like the sun from the chambers of the east, all the brighter for the night's chill darkness, while about us would be the dew of the Spirit, and the freshness of a new dawning. Sickness would be like a going into the desert to rest awhile. O that it might be so with me! My Lord, grant that it may be so, for the sake of the many people to whom these hands must yet break the bread of life.

They say that pearls are bred in the oyster by disease: may our graces be such pearls! Falling leaves enrich the soil about the forest tree: may God grant that our weeping autumns would yield us fairer springs, and larger growths. May the divine Spirit cause it so to be!

4 To increase our tenderness

Fourthly, *pain, if sanctified, creates tenderness towards others.* Alone it may harden and shut the sufferer up within himself, a student of his own nerves and ailments, and a hater of all who would rival him in suffering. But, mixed with grace, our aches and pains are a medicine which causes the milk of human kindness to fill the heart. The sick feel for the sick when their afflictions have worked in a healthy manner. One could have wished to give the gruff, unsympathetic boor a twist or two of rheumatism, were it not that our experience would make us spare even him out of pity. It is surely right to assume that they who first founded hospitals had been sick themselves, for grief has often been the mother of mercy, and the pangs of sickness the birth-throes of compassion. If our hearts learn sympathy they have been in a good school, though the Master may have used the rod most heavily, and trained by many a smart. To those who are teachers of others this is of prime importance, for none can bear with the infirmities of others if they have not been made compassionate. The keys of people's hearts hang up in the narrow chamber of suffering, and he who has not been there can scarcely know the art of opening the recesses of the soul.

The believing sufferer instinctively turns to the Lord Jesus because he has been tempted in all points like as we are. In a lesser degree the sufferer naturally looks most hopefully to those of his brethren who have most experience with infirmity, and are most familiar with anguish. Happy is the man who has been afflicted, if the Spirit shall thereby make him a son of compassion to the mourners in Zion.

5 To inspire our gratitude

Fifthly, as I find my scarcely-recovered mind cannot continue this meditation much longer, I will only add that *pain has a tendency to make us grateful when health returns*. We value the powers of locomotion after tossing long upon a bed from which we cannot rise. The open air is especially sweet after the confinement of the chamber. Food is relished when appetite returns. And in every respect, the time of recovery is one of marked enjoyment.

As birds sing most after their winter's silence, when the warm spring has newly returned, so should we give greatest praise when our gloomy hours are changed by restoration. Blessed be the Lord, who healeth all our diseases. *Jehovah Rophi* is a name much treasured by those who know the Lord who heals them. Gratitude is a choice spice for Heaven's altar. It burns well in the censer and sends up a fragrant cloud acceptable to the great High Priest.

Perhaps God would have lost much praise if his servant had not suffered much. Thus sickness yields a large tribute to the King's revenue, and as this is the case, we may cheerfully endure it. Bow down frail body and faint heart, if in so bowing you are able to yield what you had never produced standing erect in full vigour! Bruise, Lord, the spice, which otherwise would keep its sweetness slumbering and useless!

* * *

Heaven's poetry is in the agonising cry, 'Nevertheless not as I will, but as thou wilt;' and it is a grand result of trial if we learn to imitate our Lord with this hearty utterance, and thus to have fellowship with his sufferings. Here a great ocean opens up before us: pain may aid us in communion with our much-suffering Lord. Anything is a boon by which we are made more fully to be partakers with him.

Alas, we cannot now pursue the theme. As when the mariner in northern seas forces his way through an ice-blocked strait, and sees opening up before him a boundless sea, even so do we perceive great truths in our subject, but our vessel has been so tempest-tossed of late that we cannot enter on the taxing voyage, but must cast anchor under the shelter of Cape Fellowship, and leave our readers to push on into the blessed depths. May the good Spirit fill their sails, and bear them into the expanse.

The Sword and the Trowel, November 1880

6
Daniel's Band
Knowing the Special Love of God

'O Daniel, a man greatly beloved' *(Daniel 10.11)*.

I T DID NOT DO DANIEL any harm to know that he was greatly loved by God, or else he would not have received that information from Heaven. Some people are always afraid that, if Christians obtain full assurance, and receive a sweet sense of divine love, they will grow proud and be carried away with conceit. Do not have any such fear. I know of no greater blessing that can happen to any man or woman than to be assured that they are greatly loved by the Lord. Such knowledge might do us the greatest conceivable good.

It has often been said that Daniel is the John of the Old Testament, and John is the Daniel of the New Testament. Those two men, Daniel and John, were choice saints. They rose to the greatest height of spiritual obedience, and then to the greatest height of spiritual enjoyment. The knowledge that we are greatly loved by God will be a means of blessing in many ways. If we know that we are greatly loved by God we become very humble. We say, 'How could God ever love me?' I think a sense of God's love is even more humbling than a sense of our sin. When the two are blended, they sink the soul very low, not in depression of spirit, but in its estimate of itself.

A sense of God's love excites in us great gratitude. 'O!' we say, 'how can I repay the Lord for such an amazing favour?' We become conscious that we can never repay him; and we begin working out all sorts of schemes and plans to try to show how much we value the love of God. We bring out our alabaster box from its hiding-place; willingly break it, and pour the precious ointment upon the dear head of him who has loved us so greatly. I am sure that a certainty of having the love of God shed abroad in the heart by the Holy Spirit is one of the greatest promoters of holy gratitude; and holy gratitude is the mother of obedience. When we feel how much we owe, then we seek to know the will of God, and take a delight in doing it. Whatever he says to us, we are glad to do, as a proof that we really are grateful for 'love so amazing, so divine'.

This will also consecrate us. I believe that to know certainly that we are greatly loved makes us feel that we cannot live as others do. We cannot trifle with sin. They who live in the heart of the King must be faithful to him. If called to stand in God's immediate presence as courtiers and favourites, we must take care how we behave ourselves. 'Ye are not your own; for ye are bought with a price: therefore glorify God in your body, and in your spirit, which are God's.' To the degree that we are sure of his love, our love to him burns like coals of juniper, which have a most vehement heat, and everything contrary to the will of God is consumed in that blessed flame.

A sense of divine love will also strengthen us. What is there that a person will not do when in love with another person? But when we get to be in love with God, and know of his love for us, we would cut our way through a lane of devils, and face an army of demons to defeat them all, for love is a conquering grace. When faith is side by side with love, it –

> Laughs at impossibilities,
> And says, 'It shall be done!'

This assurance of God's love will make us very courageous. God makes a hero of the one on whom his love is embossed. That brother or sister will be found in the thick of the fray, defying sin, death and hell. He will burn for Christ once he is assured that he is the object of the peculiar love of God, and like Daniel can be addressed as 'a man greatly beloved'. Awareness also gives unparalleled joy. If we are greatly loved of God, how can we be miserable and discontented? If we are greatly loved, we trip with light feet over the hills of sorrow. We begin the music of Heaven even here, for a sense of God's love in the soul sets all the strings of the heart singing.

I have said all this as a preface, to show that we need not be afraid of knowing that God loves us. Some seem to think that a state of doubt is a state of discretion. It is a state of folly. Full assurance of the faithfulness and truthfulness of God is nothing but common sense spiritualised. To believe a lie is folly, but to believe the truth is wisdom. If you are a believer in Christ, though the very least and weakest of believers, you are a person greatly loved. Believe it, and be not afraid to rejoice in it. It will have no influence over you but that which is sanctifying and health-giving.

To help us think of Christ's great love to us, I am going to talk first, about *the case of Daniel*, the man greatly beloved; secondly, about *the case of every believer*; and thirdly, about *the case of some special saints*, believers who are the elect of the elect.

1 FIRST, THEN, let us consider the case of Daniel, who was 'a man greatly beloved'. Because Daniel was greatly loved of God, *he was early tried, and enabled to stand.* While he was yet a youth he was carried into Babylon, and there he refused to eat the king's meat, or to drink the king's wine. He put it to the test whether, if he

fed on common pulse, he would not be healthier and better than if he defiled himself with the king's meat.

Now, religion does not stand in meat and drink, but a good deal of irreligion does, and it may become a very important point with some as to what they eat and what they drink. Daniel was early tested, and he stood the test. He would not yield even in a small point to that which was evil. Young man, if God greatly loves you, he will give you an early test. If you are greatly loved, you will stand firm, even about so small a thing as what you eat and drink, or something even less important than that. You will say, 'I cannot sin against God. I must stand fast, even in the smallest matter, in keeping to the law of the Lord my God.' If you are enabled to do that, you are a man greatly loved.

Afterwards, Daniel *was greatly envied, but found faultless.* He was surrounded by envious enemies, who could not bear that he should be promoted over them. So they met together, and considered how they could pull him down. They were obliged to make this confession, 'We shall not find any occasion against this Daniel, except we find it against him concerning the law of his God.' Dear friend, you are greatly loved if, when your enemies meet to devise some scheme for your overthrow, they cannot say anything against you except your religion. If, when they sift you through and through, their eager, evil eyes cannot detect a fault; and they are obliged to fall back upon abusing you for your godliness, calling it hypocrisy, or some other ugly name, you are a person greatly beloved.

Further, Daniel *was delivered from great peril.* He was cast into the lions' den because he was a man greatly loved of God. I think I see some shrink back, and I hear them say, 'We do not want to go into the lions' den.' They are poor creatures, but Daniel was worth putting in the lions' den for he was big enough for the trial. Some people would be out of place among lions. Cats would be more suitable companions for them, or even mice. Even among ourselves in this Tabernacle there are many poor feeble creatures. A man preaches false doctrine and they say, 'Very good. Was it not well put?' Another preaches the Gospel, and they say, 'Very good; very good.' O, yes! it is all alike good to some, because they cannot discern between the true and the false. But Daniel could distinguish between good and evil, and therefore he was thrust into the lions' den. It was, however, a den out of which he was delivered. The lions could not eat him, for God loved him too well. The Lord preserved Daniel, and he will preserve you, dear friend, if you belong to 'Daniel's band'.

Another feature of Daniel as a man greatly beloved was that *he had revelations from God*. However, do not open your eyes with wonder, and say, 'I wish that I had all the revelations that Daniel had.' Listen to what it was like: 'I Daniel was grieved in my spirit in the midst of my body, and the visions of my head troubled me;' and again: 'As for me Daniel, my cogitations much troubled me, and my countenance changed in me: but I kept the matter in my heart.' The revelations received actually made him ill. 'I Daniel fainted, and was sick certain days; afterward I rose up, and did the king's business; and I was astonished at the vision, but none understood it.' Those whom God loves will see things that astound them, perhaps almost kill them. They will see that which will make them faint and sick well nigh unto death.

Those who are greatly beloved say, 'Let me see visions of God whatever it may cost me. Let me have communion with him even though it should break my heart, and crush me in the dust. Though it should fill me with sorrow, yet manifest thyself to me, my Lord.' Even those greatly loved, when they deal closely with God, have to find out that they are dust and ashes in his sight. They have to fall down in the presence of his glorious majesty, as the beloved John did when he fell at Christ's feet as dead.

I will make only one more remark on Daniel's case, and that is – *he stood content in his lot*. Because he was a man greatly beloved, he had this promise with which to close his marvellous book, 'Go thou thy way till the end be: for thou shalt rest, and stand in thy lot at the end of the days.' He does not understand all that God has revealed, but he is to rest quite satisfied that, when the end came, he would have his place and his portion, and he would be with his Lord for ever. The next time you get studying some prophecy of Scripture which you cannot make out, do not be troubled; but hear the voice of God saying, 'Go thy way. Wait awhile. It will all be plain in due time. God is with thee. There remains a rest for thee, a crown that no head but thine can wear, a harp that no fingers but thine can play upon, and thou shalt stand in thy lot at the end of the days.'

2 IN THE SECOND PLACE, I am going to speak of the case of every believer, who is also greatly beloved of God. Every believer has been *called out from others*. Like Abraham, you may have been called out from your family, and possibly, you do not have a converted relative. Many here are the only ones of their kith and kin that ever knew the Lord, so far as they know. See in this the sovereign, electing love of God. Are you not a person greatly beloved? Wonder at the grace of God who has called you, and be grateful. Adore him for his matchless mercy and his distinguishing grace.

Remember, too, that God loved you long before he began to deal with you in a way of grace. Before you were born, Christ died for you, and ere this world was made, God loved you with an everlasting love. Your name was in his Book; and your image was on the heart of Christ. Remember his word by the prophet Jeremiah, 'I have loved thee with an everlasting love: therefore with lovingkindness have I drawn thee.' Feed on that precious truth, inwardly digest it, let it enter into your very soul, and say, 'Surely, I may claim the title of "a man greatly beloved".'

Remember your sin for a moment. Then forget it, for God has blotted it out. He has cast all your sins behind his back, and the depths have covered them. They sank like lead in the mighty waters of oblivion, and they shall never rise to condemn you. You are forgiven. Whatever your sin, the blood of Jesus has cleansed you, and you are whiter than the snow; and he has covered you with the robe of his perfect righteousness, and you are 'accepted in the beloved'. Are you not a man greatly loved? I remember one who came creeping to the Saviour's feet. It was myself, condemned in my own conscience and expecting to be driven to the place where hope could never come. I came to Christ wearing the weeds of mourning; but, in a moment, when I looked to him, he put on me the garments of salvation. He took away my sin, he placed a fair crown upon my head, and set my feet upon a rock, and established my goings. Blessed be his name! If there is a man in the world who can sing –

> *Oh, 'twas love, 'twas wondrous love,*
> *The love of God to me!*
> *It brought my Saviour from above,*
> *To die on Calvary . . .*

I am that man; and you can sing these words too. Since the Lord forgave your sin, you have been a praying person, and God has *heard your prayers*. With the psalmist, you can say, 'Verily God hath heard me; he hath attended to the voice of my prayer.' Are you not greatly loved? We have right of entry to the King's palace at will – are we not therefore greatly loved?

Beside this, remember that the Lord has *upheld you* until now. In your pilgrim path, how many times your feet have almost gone! How often you have been tempted, and worse, how often you have yielded to temptation. Yet here you are, your character not ruined, your soul not lost, your face still toward Jerusalem, and the enemy's foot not on your neck. And it never will be, glory to the name of the Lord! When I think of all our experiences in the way in which the Lord has led us, I can truly say of all his people that they are men and women greatly loved. We are invited to *feast with Christ and his church* in the communion service, not to come as dogs under the table, but to sit with him at the royal banquet, with his banner of love waving over us. We are invited to be his companions here, his comrades at this feast. Haman thought himself honoured when he was invited to his king's banquet; but what shall we say who are bidden to come to this much, much higher festival?

Only one thing more will I say under this heading, but this story is so marvellous, that we may be for ever telling it, and yet it will never all be told. The love of Christ to some of us has been so wonderful, that when we once begin the theme, we seem to forget all about time, and wish there were no fleeting hours to bid us end our narrative! *We shall be with him soon.* Some of us sit here heavy at heart; and there are wrinkles on the brow, and there is a weariness in the frame which makes the wheels of life drag heavily. Beloved, it is but the twinkling of an eye, so brief is life, and we shall be with him where he is, and shall behold his glory. Do you ever try to realise the greatness of that love that will take you to be with Christ, to dwell with him, and to share his glory for ever? Can you put the incorruptible crown on your head now in your imagination (or rather, in faith)? Can you, even now, begin to wave the palm of victory, and strike the harp of everlasting praise? Do you feel as if you could, even now, join the sacred throng above, and sing the heavenly hymn of the ages yet to be? As surely as we are in Christ tonight, we shall be with Christ by-and-by. O, men and women greatly loved, to have such a future as this before you, ought to make your Heaven begin below!

3 FINALLY I MUST SPEAK of the case of special saints, those who are in a peculiar sense people greatly beloved. There are some who are, as I said at the beginning of my discourse, elect out of the elect. Remember, that Christ had seventy choice men, his disciples, but then he had twelve choicer men, his apostles, and he had three of these who were with him when the others were not, and out of these three he had one, John, that 'disciple, whom Jesus loved'.

His love is so sweet, that, while I would be grateful to be even outside the seventy, so long as I might be among the five hundred brethren who saw him after he rose from the dead, yet I would then have the ambition to get in among the seventy. And not for the honour of it, but for the love it would bring, I would like to be one of the eleven. And for the same reason I would like to be one of the three. And I would be thankful beyond words to be that one whom Jesus loved. Have you not the same holy aspiration? Well, now, let me tell you that, if you desire to be among the choicer spirits, exceptionally loved of God, you must be *people of spotless character*. Christ loves great sinners, and even saints that fall and stain their garments he will not cast away; but we will never *enjoy* the fulness of Christ's love unless we keep our garments unspotted from the world.

You cannot find a fault in Daniel; and if you want to live on earth so as to be in Heaven while you are here, and to drink the wine of Christ's love to the bottom of the chalice, you must watch every step, and observe every word; for our Lord is very jealous, and half a word of evil will grieve him. If you would walk in the light as he is in the light, and have constant fellowship with God, I beseech you, be ye perfect, even as your Father which is in Heaven is perfect, and follow after unsullied holiness. The pure in heart shall see God. O, that everyone might have this purity! It is those who have not defiled their garments who shall walk with Christ in white.

The next point is, that men who are greatly beloved are *men of decision*. When Daniel had the lions' den in prospect, because of his faithfulness to his God, 'he went into his house; and his windows being open in his chamber toward Jerusalem, he kneeled upon his knees three times a day, and prayed, and gave thanks before his God, as he did aforetime.' There was no compromising in Daniel's case. If you want to be greatly loved, do not attempt any compromise with sin. Have nothing to do with craftiness, holding with the true and the false at the same time. If God is to use you in his service, you must be like the tribe of Levi, separate from your brethren, and you must ever be ready to stand up bravely for God and for his eternal Truth at any cost. It is my earnest desire that we may have in this church many men and women of this kind, who will be out and out for Christ.

Next, if you would be men greatly beloved of God on whom special shinings of his face shall come, you must be *much in communion with him*. Daniel fasted and prayed, and communed with God with cries and tears, and God came and revealed himself to him. He was greatly beloved, for he lived near to God. He was no far-off follower of his Lord. He dwelt in the full blaze of the Sun of Righteousness. If a man is to be greatly loved of God, he must *live above the world*, as Daniel did. Daniel became a prince, a governor, a man of substance and position, but when Belshazzar promised to clothe him with scarlet, and to put a gold chain about his neck, he said to the king, 'Let thy gifts be to thyself, and give thy rewards to another.' Daniel did not want them.

When he became great in the land, he walked with God as he had done when he was poor. It is a dangerous thing for some people to be made much of in the world. Their heads soon get turned, and they begin to think too much of themselves. He who thinks that he is somebody is nobody, and he whose head begins to swim because of his elevation, will soon have it broken because of his tumbling down from his lofty position. Daniel was a man greatly beloved, and God showed his great love to him by setting him in high places, and keeping him there in safety.

Once more, men who are greatly loved by the Lord *live wholly for God and for God's people*. You see nothing of selfishness about Daniel. He neither seeks to be great nor to be rich. He loves his own people, and he pleads with God for the seed of Abraham. If you want to be greatly beloved, give yourselves up to the service of God and his church. To stand alone for God in such an evil age as this, is a great honour. How few care to swim against the strong stream running in opposition to the Truth of God. If you are loyal to Christ and his infallible Word, prove it now. Then shall you hear him say to you also, 'O man greatly beloved, go thou thy way till the end be: for thou shalt rest, and stand in thy lot at the end of the days.'

Edited from a sermon preached by C. H. Spurgeon in 1890

7
The Day Shall Declare It
The Great Day of Judgement

'The day shall declare it' *(1 Corinthians 3.13)*.

TIME IS A SEARCHING TEST of earthly things. Empires once thought substantial as granite, have melted in the lapse of ages like foam upon the waters. Philosophies which appeared to be utterly sure have proved to be fictions, no more enduring than grass mown down and cast into the oven. Even religions which commanded the faith or fear of millions have passed away like phantoms of the night. The gods of one century are the demons of the next. In all things mortal, time writes change, and brings decay. Time rusts the bars of prisons, and frets the palaces of kings. Nothing escapes his devouring teeth. The test of time will also be brought to bear on all *our* actions, and if we seek to build things which will endure, we need to be very careful as to the foundation, the materials, and the method of our building.

In addition to the test of time, a severer test is to come at the end of time, when the day for which all other days were made shall arrive. Then that fire which ever consumes the wood, hay, and stubble, will be blown up to a still more vehement heat, for 'the day cometh, that shall burn as an oven'. Then will come the ultimate test of all. Then every evil thought, motive, principle, act, and word, shall be detected and unmasked. 'The day shall declare it,' for in that day 'the fire shall try every man's work of what sort it is.' It is of that great trial day that I wish now to speak, but I must speak with stammering lips on such a theme as this. It is too great, too weighty for human language ever to convey to you the fulness of its solemnity.

My first theme will be, *how different eyes will view this great day of declaration.* When it will come, we do not know: 'Of that day and that hour knoweth no man, no, not the angels which are in heaven.' But as a thief, unheard, unseen, it steals on us. It may be much nearer than we think, or it may be much more remote than some would have us believe. But come it will to every one of us, and we shall all take part in the proceedings of that day, not merely as spectators, but as participants.

The vindication of believers

To some eyes, that day will come with brightness as *a day of justification.* They have been for many years trusting in Christ and seeking to do his will, and, because of this, they have been accused of foolishness. They have lost (it has been thought) much allowable pleasure. Indeed, it has been suggested that they have made a terrible mistake, because they have suffered for Christ's sake. Many followers of Christ have been in prison, and others have been stoned or have yielded up their bodies to be burned for the sake of things which they could not see, and which other men derided. When that last day shall come, they will be fully justified for this supposed folly. Then shall it be seen that they did the right and true and noble and best thing, and even the most judicious thing for their own welfare. It shall then be discovered that it was better to suffer for the Truth than to enjoy the pleasures of falsehood, and that it was a greater gain, in the long run, to endure reproach for Christ's sake than to accept all the honours and all the treasures of Egypt.

Those who were reckoned fools will be accounted wise in that day. Those who were regarded as the off-scouring of all things will then be esteemed as 'the precious sons of Zion, comparable to fine gold', and the acclamations of all angels will accord them the highest honours, and the wicked, by their sullen silence, will be compelled to confess that the righteous were right after all. In that day, there will be a resurrection of reputations as well as of bodies, and the slandered saint shall come forth, like the sun from behind the clouds, and shine with the greater radiance because of its temporary eclipse.

That day will also be, to the saints, *a day of great consolation.* There will be great disclosures of secrets and mysteries made to them on that last, revealing day. You remember how our Lord said to Peter, 'What I do thou knowest not now; but thou shalt know hereafter;' and then will the godly understand why they were persecuted, and how good it was for them to suffer affliction with Christ. Then will some of them see the reason for their poverty, and others will learn why they suffered the loss of all things. Then will some understand the reason for those sicknesses which often deprived them of opportunities of usefulness, and others will see why they were tempted of Satan, and why they had to dwell among ungodly men and women. Then will they learn the reason for all the difficulties through which they had to enter the kingdom.

I believe that when this revelation bursts upon the righteous at the last great day they will be overwhelmed with astonishment at the infinite lovingkindness of God in their afflictions. They will then say, with David, 'I will sing of mercy and judgment: unto thee, O Lord, will I sing.' This mortal life is often a tangle, and we cannot unravel it. It is a puzzle and a mystery. We see the wicked prospering, and the righteous chastened every morning. But then we shall see the reason for every stroke of the rod, and for every blast of the furnace; and we shall understand that the Lord dealt graciously with his servants after all.

Further, that day will be to the righteous *a most confirming day.* They believed in God on earth; but, oh! what solid grounds they will then see for their faith! When they saw but through a glass darkly, they felt that it was right to trust in the living God, and in his Son, whom he had revealed from Heaven; but when they shall see Jesus face to face, when the great Sun of Righteousness shall shine brightly before their mortal eyes, they will exclaim – 'Now we know, of a surety, that the half has not been told us. We were assured, on earth, that Christ was precious; but how precious is he now! We heard, on earth, that God was just; but see how just he is, as we behold him on the great white throne. When we were down below, we were told, in the great Book of God, and by his ministers, that they who trusted in him should never be confounded. We found that to be true even on earth, but we find it to be still more true here, for no tongue that once rose against us in judgement stands uncondemned. We are, indeed, absolved and acquitted in this last tremendous day.'

It will be a great blessing that you will not, in that day, have to cast aside all you learned on earth. You will learn more concerning the Truth, but you will not have to learn a new Gospel. The great fundamentals of the faith, on which your soul now rests, will stand as firmly throughout eternity as they do today. The substitution of Christ will still be your joy; the covenant of grace will still be your comfort; the everlasting love of God will still be your Heaven. That which you loved on earth, you shall love then. That which was your comfort on earth, shall be your comfort then. You shall not need to leave the good old road, which your fathers trod.

What acclamations of adoration will the righteous give in that day. They will rejoice with exceeding joy, and their enlarged capacities will enable their bodies and souls together to hold greater bliss. Thinking of all this, we may long for that day.

The loss of unbelievers

But that day will wear quite another aspect to those who are not in Christ. I would speak to them very earnestly, and with deep affection. Friend, if you live and die without a Saviour, *that day will clothe you with unutterable shame.* You will say to yourself, 'What a fool I was to live for a world that has now gone from me! What a madman I was to choose the little transient happiness that sin gave me, and to forget all about the great assize, and the verdict of that Judge who now cries to the ungodly, "Depart from me, ye cursed!" '

Then will remorse come to you without relief, and your own conscience will join in accusing you. I tell the greatest and richest of you that, if you are found without Christ, you will wish that you had been the meanest pauper that ever died in a workhouse, if you might have had a Saviour. Kings will disdain their crowns, and princes wish their honours to be trampled in the mire, desiring that they might rather have been like Lazarus lying at the rich man's gate full of sores if, after all, they might but have had a portion amongst the blessed.

Then they who said, 'Let us eat and drink; for to morrow we die,' will be worse off than the beasts that perish; and they, who defiantly asked, 'Who is the Lord, that we should obey him?' will seem to be monsters of folly. They who said, 'There is neither angel, nor spirit, nor resurrection,' shall know the truth of all they denied, and they shall find themselves promoted into shame, for 'shame shall be the promotion of fools'. With this shame shall come *convicting power.* Some disbelieve, or pretend to disbelieve, in the existence of God, and truths revealed in Scripture, but that great day will banish all infidelity. When he shall come, every man shall discover that he is in God's power, and that he must stand face to face with his Creator.

There will be no atheism, and no more theism either, for he who sits upon the throne will be Jesus of Nazareth, the Son of God, and all who despised and refused him shall tremble at the sight of his face, and desire to be hidden from it. That face will convince them in a moment, better than all our arguments and reasonings, for the eyes and ears of the ungodly shall convince them, and the fact that they have been raised from their graves shall convince them that God is God, and his judgement is about to be passed on them.

But, alas, that day will bring to them *a state of confusion* as well as of conviction. You remember that man, who did not wear a wedding garment, and who stood speechless before the king? What else could he do? I can think of many reasons with which a man can stultify his conscience, but I cannot think of one that he would have the audacity to bring out in the light of that tremendous day. No, speechless he must be, for he will know that the justice of God cannot err, and that, if the thunderbolts of the Almighty fall upon him, it will be just. No matter how strongly he may wish to clear himself, yet he will not be able to answer for one sin out of a thousand. He must, by his silence, plead guilty to all, and own the justice of the sentence which will follow.

This last great day will wear a truly awful aspect to all who are out of Christ, for their conviction and their confusion will be followed by *their condemnation*. Why, possibly within a few months, or a few years at the outside, we shall all have passed into the realm of spirits; and however long or short the interval may be, 'we shall all stand before the judgment seat of Christ.' It will not then seem to be a trivial matter, when you wake up from the grave, and find yourself without a hope, without a Saviour, naked before your God, and driven for ever from his presence. Give heed to these things. Do not fling away your souls, and make your eternal destiny to be one of unbroken wretchedness. Ask God deeply to impress eternal things upon your thoughtful hearts, and even now to give you the grace to repent of all your sin, and to trust the merits of his Son.

Aspects of judgement day

Now, let us think, for a little while, *how different things will bear the test of that great day of declaration*. What a mass of *professions* will be brought to the test on that day! Here we are, some thousands of professing Christians, who have been avowedly baptised into Christ. Some of our professions, when put into the fire, will come out as they went in – solid, substantial, golden professions. Will that be your case? Preacher, will that be your case? Hearer, will it be yours?

On the other hand, there will be some professions which look very golden now, but which will begin to shrivel almost before they reach the fire. The gilded public demeanour will curl up, and disappear, and that person's profession will be detected to have been mere tinsel and counterfeit. Will that be your case, my friend? We did our best, when we received you into church fellowship, to judge the truth of your profession.

Since then, you have done your best to maintain the outward morality which is required of a professing Christian. But were you ever born again? Were you ever really converted? That question none of us can answer; you yourself must judge the matter, and in that judgement you will need the Lord to be your Helper. Therefore, pray the prayer of the psalmist, 'Search me, O God, and know my heart: try me, and know my thoughts: and see if there be any wicked way in me, and lead me in the way everlasting.'

Reputations, too, will be tested on that last, tremendous day. On earth, reputations go very much according to success or wealth. I have seen men who have been admitted into all classes of society as most reputable persons, yet those who knew them well, knew that their money was not gained in a right way. They were frauds, perhaps, or they grew rich on the tears of widows, who were made such by the liquor these men sold.

There is many a man who is reckoned respectable because of his money, yet every farthing of it was coined in the mint of hell, and came to him directly through the damnation of the souls of others. That last, tremendous day will shrivel up some famous men. There are many who have been knighted, but their method of business could not be proclaimed upon the housetops. Some of your great men – how small will they become in that day. I almost wish it were already come, for the infamies of this city cry to God to hasten the hour when he shall in righteousness draw up the curtain, and let the wicked be known to be wicked, and the churl to be a churl, and the oppressor to be an oppressor.

Your eloquent preacher, also, who spoke so well, but who lived so ill; your fine orator who was so great at telling others how they should live, but who did not live so himself; your professing Christian, who was pious in church or chapel, who sat regularly at the Lord's Table, but who, meanwhile, was at home a despot and a tyrant, unforgiving, unrelenting – how the fine feathers will be pulled off these fine birds; and what a come-down there will be for them!

In that day, too, there will be a testing of *positions*. There will be first who shall be last, and last who shall be first. There will be a testing also of *boastings* and those who now talk loudly and proudly will be dumb; while those who now are silent shall sing out for joy. Talk of 'turning the world upside down', this will indeed be accomplished in the day when God shall judge the world in righteousness by Christ Jesus.

I pray that we may have nothing about us that need dread the fire. May we be free from shams and hypocrisies. May we be clear as the morning light, straight as an arrow. May we be consistently truthful in thought, word, and deed. And even should mistakes arise – as they will, for we are frail – let us never forget that the blood of Christ is prepared to remove the guilt of those mistakes, and when the great testing time shall come, we, having been saved by our Redeemer's sacrifice, shall stand forth, clear as the sun, accepted before the throne of God.

How should this affect us?

Now I come to the last point of my discourse, which is this – *in what ways a consideration of this great day ought to affect us all.*

First, *it ought to startle some of us*, for 'the day shall declare it'. If there be any hearer who has some secret transgression in which he or she is still living, if you are not discovered *now,* you will be *then.* I do pity some inconsistent Christians who have lived for years like debtors hunted by a bailiff, always afraid of being discovered. But they should have been more afraid of God, since he knows all, records all, and will publish all on the last day, if it be not blotted out by the precious blood of Jesus Christ. This ought to startle every sinner who is still in his sins.

Certainly, all unrenewed hearts ought to begin to tremble. You are unsaved, though outwardly excellent in other respects, yet you are unsaved! Young man, with much about you that we can commend, you are yet unsaved, and that day will reveal to the world your unforgiven sin. You will have no robe of righteousness to wear. You will have no fountain full of cleansing blood to wash away your guilt. What will you do amidst the terrors of that last, great day? I plead with all who have not Christ as their Saviour, to seek him now.

The way of salvation is very simple; it is just this. Jesus Christ suffered in the room, and place, and stead of as many as will trust him. If you trust him, it is certain that all your sins were laid upon him, that he suffered all that you ought to have suffered on their account, that you are forgiven for his sake, and that you shall never be condemned, for 'he that believeth on him is not condemned.' Why don't you believe in him now? I have no greater joy, out of Heaven, than when I hear of those who commit themselves to Christ. Never a day passes but that I hear of those who find peace with God under the Gospel. I wonder how long it will be before you, dear hearer, to whom I have preached these many years, will be added to the happy throng of those who are resting in Christ.

A day or two ago, I had a letter from one who says, 'I heard you preach, in a certain street, some twelve years ago,' and he brings to my recollection the subject of my discourse. It was about being almost persuaded to be a Christian. He was a youth then; but the Truth stuck in his conscience, wounded him, and led him to come to Christ. He wrote to tell me that, in the class which he is teaching in the Sunday School, ten boys have been brought to Christ, and added to the church, and now he himself has become a deacon of the church, and he thought it was time that he made me a partaker of his joy, by letting me know how he was brought to Christ. It was only once that I preached there, yet that soul was won, but I have preached to some of you hundreds of times, yet you do not come to Christ. Oh, when will the fire dissolve the rock? O blessed Spirit, do save these my hearers yet! Let them not be cast away in that last day that shall declare it; but may they even now lay hold on eternal life, and be saved!

My last word is to you who believe in Christ. It is – 'Wait.' If you are a true Christian, you will be sure to be misrepresented, you will be sure to be slandered, but 'the day shall declare it,' so wait! I believe we never do worse business than when we try to set ourselves right before unbelieving people. Let them lie about us, if they will; and let them misjudge us, if they please. We are no servants of theirs; we serve a higher Master, before whom we shall stand or fall. They call you 'hypocrite'. 'The day shall declare it.' They say that you are officious and proud, because you are zealous and earnest. 'The day shall declare it.' Wait! Be not in a hurry. The day of your deliverance is at hand; the Judge is even at the door. Bear the reproaches of the ungodly, endure their oppressions, hold yourself still, and bide your time; for the day of recompensing when the wrongs are righted, will be worth waiting for. Think of when we shall 'see the king in his beauty,' and shall be like him, and shall hear him say, 'Well done, good and faithful servant'! This day shall for ever shut the mouth of calumny, and make the face of slander to turn pale and die. God bless you; and may you be 'looking for and hasting unto the coming of the day of God'! 'Be ye also ready: for in such an hour as ye think not the Son of man cometh.'

An edited sermon of C. H. Spurgeon, published posthumously in
The Sword and the Trowel, January 1901 (not in *Metropolitan Tabernacle Pulpit*)

8

Be Not Weary in Well Doing

An Address to the Metropolitan Tabernacle Ladies' Working
Benevolent Society

Before the dawn of the welfare state, believers often bore the burden of
community social relief. In Spurgeon's time the Tabernacle was a 'working
church' in all respects, and this message to only one of the work groups
provides a small insight into this.

I HAVE SO OFTEN spoken to you upon various aspects of your
good work, that I thought, on this occasion, I would take a few
of the apostle Paul's words as a sort of peg on which to hang my
remarks. You will find the passage in *Galatians 6.9*: 'Let us not be
weary in well doing: for in due season we shall reap, if we faint not.'

Your benevolent work, dear sisters, is one of the kinds of well
doing in which people do grow weary. I have no doubt that a good
deal of weariness comes of that perpetual stitch, stitch, stitch, and of
your efforts to minister to the poor and needy ones who abound in
this neighbourhood. There is Mrs Brown over there (the mother of
our dear brother Harry Brown, of Darjeeling). I should think she is

sometimes weary, for she always seems to be busy all day long about some good work or other; and there are many other earnest, godly women here, of her stamp, always at work for the Lord. It is not surprising if, sometimes, they are as tired as if they had been toiling all day at the carpenter's bench, or out in the fields following the plough. Physical weariness will come on; yet that is not being weary of the work, but weary in it; and that weariness may sometimes be the part of the sacrifice which is most acceptable to God. We cannot offer to our Lord that which costs us nothing, and its preciousness in his sight will often be in exact proportion to the costliness of the service.

I think that we grow weary *of* well doing, and *in* well doing, *when there seems to be no end to it;* and there is no end to such work as yours in this terrible London, especially at such a time as this. All that you can do is but as a drop in the bucket of the privation and distress around you. All the garments that you make, all the food and money that you give, go but a very little way towards relieving the wants of this awfully overgrown city. Still, do not give up because you can do so little, and because your work seems of such small use. You little coral insects must go on with your unobserved labours, piling up the rocks upon which the next succession of workers will have to build, and by-and-by, as the result of such toil as yours, there will be a beautiful island of refuge formed amid the stormy sea of London's poverty and sorrow.

We are also apt to get weary in well doing *when the persons whom we help do not seem to be grateful for what we do for them.* There is a great deal of ingratitude in the world. But if you, my good sisters, will never expect any thanks for what you do, and if you do not wonder when you meet with ingratitude, and if you remember how ungrateful you have yourselves been for all the goodness of God to you; then, all the gratitude that *does* come will be a sweet surprise, and all the more welcome because you did not look for it, or expect it. But, anyhow, let us not stay our hand from doing good because the people we help are ungrateful for all that is done for them. Thus shall we show that we are true children of our Father in Heaven, who 'is kind unto the unthankful and to the evil'.

And again, do not let us be weary in well doing *because sometimes our well doing is turned to bad account.* What if the sixpences that we give in charity are wickedly spent upon gin? What if the money that we bestow for a loaf of bread is spent upon beer? It is a very evil thing when that is the case; and, as a teetotaller, I wish the people would all give up the drink, and drop their drop of beer; but, at the same time, I do not think that I am responsible for their perversion of my gifts. If poor people come to me, apparently starving, and I give them bread, and when they receive it, they turn it into drink, I am not to be held accountable for their wrongdoing. My present and pressing duty is to relieve the hungry, and to prevent starvation as far as I can. If men and women are so sinful as to abuse the mercy which God sends to them through me, I am not to be so wrong as to cease from giving to the poor on that account.

If God were to keep back from us all his mercies because we might turn them into evils, there would be very little for him to bestow upon us. There is not anything in this world, however good it may be, but may be turned to evil by the sons of men; but God does not withhold his favours because of that sad fact. Robert Hall used to say that it was a distinguishing mark of the goodness of God that we were ever allowed to eat apple pie after the Fall! The Lord has not withered all our gardens, nor dried up all our fountains, nor for ever turned all our pastures into a wilderness, because of sin. The world remains a place of exceeding beauty, and a storehouse of wondrous joy, notwithstanding all the sin that has marred that perfect creation of God.

But, oftentimes, there is an occasion of *weariness arising from our work not being recognised.* I remember certain disappointed workers who once said, very sorrowfully, 'Our service is not appreciated as it ought to be; we are quite ignored.' How often I have wished that people would ignore me, and especially that I might be ignored by the postman and the letter writers! Oh, Harrald *[Spurgeon's personal secretary]*, you and I would be almost in Heaven if we could be out of the reach of letters, and telegrams, with requests for sermons and speeches that we cannot possibly deliver, piteous appeals for the loan of money, and entreaties that we would try to settle quarrels, or help to manage certain good men and women, who are very difficult to control when they get wrong!

I have occasionally heard that bitter complaint, 'I have worked on now for many years, and I have not had a word of encourage-ment or approval spoken to me, and there's Mrs So-and-so, quite a newcomer, see what a fuss is made of her and her work!' Do you know, my dear sisters, that the best work at the Tabernacle is that about which I hardly ever hear anything? As long as I do not hear anything about the work of a Society, I know it is going on all right; for whenever there is a screw loose, I generally hear of it pretty soon. You good ladies, keep on doing your work for the Lord, and if we do not commend you for it, as we really ought, it is because we do not know anything that we can say that would be good enough to express our appreciation of the service you are rendering to the church and to the world.

I dare not begin to mention the names of the ladies who have been serving the Lord and helping the poor through this Society, for they would shake their heads, dear souls, and look at me through their eye-glasses, and say, 'Do leave off, and let us alone; that kind of talk ought not to be uttered. We do not want it, and we do not care to hear it.' They are quite satisfied in having done their duty, and ministered to their Lord, and they will be perfectly content if he condescends to accept their service. If any of you ever do complain that nobody praises you for what you do; if you only let me know, I will enquire into the matter, and very soon set the whole thing right, but I do not expect to have any such task as that. No, no, you do not want anything of that sort; you are grateful to have had the privilege of ministering to the poor, and you willingly leave all commendation of your work to your dear Lord and Master, who will never forget the smallest service rendered to anyone 'for his sake'.

I do, however, thank every lady here for all that she has done in connection with this Society, and I thank those who are yet to come, who will be brought in by you to do similar service during the coming year. I leave my text with you, taking it to myself as I give it to you – 'Let us not be weary in well doing: for in due season we shall reap, if we faint not.' You have done well, you are doing well; and you must try to do even better in the future than you have done in the past. May the Lord abundantly bless the Metropolitan Tabernacle Ladies' Working Benevolent Society, for Christ's sake! Amen.

9
'Battlements' or Spiritual Parapets
The Rules of Spiritual Safety

This message from *Deuteronomy* supplies a masterly example of
'spiritualisation' as employed by Puritan and Victorian preachers.

IN *DEUTERONOMY 22.8* WE MEET with an interesting law
which in its letter was binding on the Jewish people, and in its
spirit furnishes an admirable rule for us upon whom the ends
of the earth are come: 'When thou buildest a new house, then thou
shalt make a battlement for thy roof, that thou bring not blood upon
thine house, if any man fall from thence.'

It is hardly necessary to inform readers that the roofs of Eastern
dwellings were flat, and that the inhabitants were accustomed
to spending much of their time on them, talking during the day,
and sleeping at night. If their roofs were without any fencing or
protection around the edge, it might often happen that little children would fall off, and grown-ups also might inadvertently take
a false step and suffer serious injury. Where there were no railings

or low walls around the roof accidents frequently occurred, and so God commanded his people while they were still in the wilderness, that when they came into the promised land and proceeded to build houses, they should take care in every case to build an adequate railing. No man has a right to do anything which must inevitably lead to the death or to the injury of those by whom he is surrounded, but he is bound to do all in his power to prevent any harm coming to his fellow men. That seems to be the moral teaching of this ordinance.

But if ordinary life is precious, how much more is the life of the soul. Therefore it is our Christian duty never to do anything which imperils either our own or other men's souls. To us there is an imperative call from the great Master that we both care for the eternal interests of others, and that, so far as we can, we prevent their exposure to temptations which might lead to a fatal fall into sin.

We shall now lead you to a few meditations which have, in our mind, gathered around this text. God has battlemented his own house. Let this serve as a great truth with which to begin our thinking. God takes care that all his children are safe. There are many high places in his house, and he does not deny his children the enjoyment of these high places, but he makes sure that they shall not be in danger there. He sets a balcony round about them lest they should suffer some calamity when in a state of exaltation.

God in his house has given us *many high and sublime doctrines*. Timid minds are afraid of these, but the highest doctrine in Scripture may be perfectly safe because God has battlemented it. Just as no man need be afraid in the East to walk on the roof of his house when the battlement is in position, so no man need hesitate to believe the doctrine of election, the doctrine of eternal and immutable love, or any of the divine teachings which circle around the covenant of grace. Take for instance the doctrine of election. What a high and glorious truth this is, that God has from the beginning chosen his people unto salvation through sanctification of the Spirit and the belief of the Truth! Yet that doctrine has turned many simpletons dizzy through looking at it *without its allied teachings*. Some have wilfully leaped over the battlement which God has set about this doctrine, and have turned it into Antinomianism, degrading it into an excuse for evil living, and reaping just damnation for their wilful perversion. But God has been pleased to set around that doctrine other truths which (when left in position) shield it from abuse.

It is true he has a chosen people, but Scripture says that it is 'by their fruits ye shall know them. Without holiness no man shall see the Lord.' Though he has chosen his people, yet he has chosen them 'unto holiness'; he has ordained them to be 'zealous of good works'. His intention is not that they should be saved *in* their sins, but saved *from* their sins; not that they should be carried to Heaven as they are, but that they should be cleansed and purged from all iniquities, and so made meet to be partakers of the inheritance of the saints in light.

Then there is the sublime truth of the final perseverance of the saints. What a noble height is that! A housetop doctrine indeed! What a view is to be had from the summit of it! It would be a great loss to us if we were unable to enjoy the comfort of this truth. There is no reason for fearing presumption through a firm conviction of the true believer's safety. Mark well the battlements which God has built around the edge of this truth. We read warnings such as – 'Let him that thinketh he standeth take heed lest he fall' – and we see how God has made a parapet around this tower-like truth, so that saints may ascend to its very summit, and look abroad upon the land that floweth with milk and honey, and yet their brains need not whirl, nor shall they fall into presumption and perish.

That wonderful doctrine of justification by faith, which we all hold to be a vital truth, is quite as dangerous by itself as the doctrine of election. In fact, if a man means to sin, he can break down every bulwark and turn any doctrine into an apology for transgression. The battlement to the doctrine of justification by faith is *the necessity of sanctification*. Where faith is genuine, through the Holy Spirit's power, it works a cleansing from sin, a hatred of evil, an anxious desire after holiness, and it leads the soul to aspire after the image of God. Faith and holiness are inseparable. 'If any man be in Christ, he is a new creature.' Good works are to be insisted on, for they have their essential purpose. James never contradicts Paul after all; it is only that we do not understand him. Both the doctrinal Paul and the practical James spoke as they were moved of the Holy Ghost. Paul builds the tower and James puts the battlement around it.

Let us consider some of the other battlements which the Lord puts around our Christian lives. The Lord *guards the position of his saints when endowed with wealth.* Some of God's servants are, in his providence, called to prosperous circumstances in life, but prosperity is full of dangers. It is hard to carry a full cup without a spill. Yet we may be well assured that if God calls any to be prosperous, and places him in an eminent position, he will see to it that suitable grace is given *and* the necessary affliction for that elevation.

The Lord will put battlements round his child, and these will certainly not commend themselves to our carnal instincts. Things will seem to be going along very nicely when we will somehow be brought to a dead stop. We will kick against this hindering disappointment, but it will not move out of our way. We shall be vexed with it, but there it will remain. Oh, how anxious we will be to go a step further, for then – or so we think – we will be supremely happy. But it is precisely that 'perfect happiness' so nearly within reach that God will not permit us to attain, for then we would receive our portion in this life, forget our God, and despise the better land.

That bodily infirmity, that sick child, that suffering wife, that embarrassing partnership – any one of these may be the battlement which God has built around our success, lest we should be lifted up with pride, and our souls should not be alive and healthy in us. Does not this 'battlement principle' cast a light upon the mystery of many a painful providence? 'Before I was afflicted I went astray: but now have I kept thy word.'

The same care is manifested by our Lord towards those whom he has seen fit to place in *positions of eminent service*. Those who express great concern for prominent ministers, because of their temptations, do well, but they will be even more in the path of duty if they have as much solicitude about themselves. I remember one whose pride was visible in his very manner. He was a person unknown, of little service in the church, but as proud of his little badly-ploughed, weedy half acre, as ever a man could be. He informed me very pompously on more than one occasion that he trembled lest I should be unduly exalted and puffed up with pride. Now, from his lips, it sounded like comedy, and reminded me of Satan reproving sin.

God never honours his servants with success without effectually preventing their grasping the honour of their work. If we are tempted to boast he soon lays us low. He always whips behind the door at home those whom he most honours in public. You may rest assured that if God honours you to win many souls, you will have many stripes to bear, and stripes you would not like to tell another of, they will be so sharp and humbling. If the Lord loves you, he will never let you be lifted up in his service.

Do not shrink from preparing yourself for the most eminent position, or from occupying it when duty calls. Do not let Satan deprive God's cause of your best service through your bashfulness. The Lord will give his angels charge over you to keep you in all your ways. If God sets you on the housetop, he will place a battlement round about you. It is the same with regard to the high places of *spiritual enjoyment*. Paul was caught up to the third heaven, and he heard words unlawful for a man to utter: this was a very high, a very, very high place for Paul's mind, mighty brain and heart as he had; but then, there was the battlement – 'Lest I should be exalted above measure through the abundance of the revelations, there was given to me a thorn in the flesh, the messenger of Satan to buffet me.' The temptation, if we are happy in the Lord, is to grow secure. 'My mountain standeth firm,' we say, 'I shall never be moved.' Even much communion with Christ, though in itself sanctifying, may be perverted into a cause of self-security.

Thus it is that just as surely as we have high seasons of enjoyment we shall sooner or later endure periods of deep depression. Scarcely ever is there a profound calm on the soul's sea, without a storm is brewing. Lest the soul should be beguiled to live upon itself, and feed on its frames and feelings, and by neglect of watchfulness fall into presumptuous sins, battlements are set round about all hallowed joys, for which (in eternity) we shall bless the name of the Lord.

From the fact of divine care, we proceed by an easy step to the effect of the commandment upon our conduct: in a word, *we ought to have our own houses battlemented.* Those who profess to be the children of God should, for their own sakes, see that every care is used to guard themselves against the perils of this tempted life. They should see to it that their house is carefully battlemented. Every man ought to examine himself carefully whether he be in the faith, lest professing too much, taking too much for granted, he should fall and perish.

At times we should close our spiritual 'wardrobe' and take stock. A tradesman who does not like to do that is generally in a bad way. We must do this lest we should, after all, be hypocrites or self-deceivers; lest, after all, we should not be born again, but should be children of nature, neatly dressed, but not the living children of God. We must prove our own selves whether we be in the faith. Let us protect our soul's interest with frequent self-examination.

Better still, and safer by far, *go often to the cross*, as we may imagine we went at first. Go every day to the cross, still with the empty hand and with the bleeding heart. Go and receive everything from Christ and seek to have your wounds bound up with the healing ointment of his atoning sacrifice. These are the best battlements I can recommend you: self-examination on the one side of the house, and a simple faith in Jesus on the other.

Be sure that you battlement yourself about *with much watchfulness,* and especially, *watch most the temptation peculiar to your situation in life and your personality.* You may not be inclined to be lazy; you may not be fascinated by the silver of Demas into covetousness, and yet you may be beguiled by pleasure. Watch, if you have a hasty temper, lest that should overthrow you; or, if yours be a high and haughty spirit, set a double watch to bring *that* demon down. If you be inclined to indolence, or, on the other hand, if hot passions or evil desires are most likely to attack you, cry to the strong Lord for strength; and as he who guards well sets a double guard where the wall is weakest, so must you.

There are some respects in which every man should battlement his house by denying himself some pleasures which might be lawful to others, but which would prove fatal to himself. Every man, I believe, has a particular sin which is a sin to him but may not be a sin to another. No man's conscience is to be a judge for another, but let no man violate his own conscience.

As each man ought to battlement his house in a spiritual sense with regard to himself, *so ought each man to carry out the rule with regard to his family.* Do maintain family religion, and never let the altar of God burn low in your home. The same applies in the matter of family discipline. If the child shall do everything he chooses to do, and if there is no admonition, if the reins be loosely held, if the father altogether neglects to be a spiritual guide and ruler in his house, how can he wonder that his children one by one grow up to break his heart? David never chastised Absalom, nor Adonijah, and remember what they became. Eli's sons never had more than a soft word or two from their father. Battlement your houses by godly discipline; see that obedience be maintained, and that sin is not tolerated, then shall your house be holiness unto the Lord, and peace shall dwell within.

We ought strictly to battlement our houses *because of the very many evils which are tolerated in this day.* I am sometimes asked, 'May a Christian subscribe to a lottery? May a Christian indulge in a game of cards? May a Christian dance or attend the opera?' Now I shall not comment upon the absolute right or wrong of debatable amusements and customs. The fact is, that if professors do not stop till they are certainly in the wrong, they will stop nowhere. It is of little use going on until you are over the edge of the roof, and then calling, 'Stop!' It would be a poor affair for a house to be without a battlement, but to have a net half-way down to stop people falling. The line had better be drawn too soon than too late.

We should carefully discern between places of public amusement. Some are perfectly harmless, recreational and instructive – to deny these to our young people would be foolish; but certain amusements stand on the border land between the openly profane and the really harmless. We say, do not go to these; never darken the doors of such places. Why? Because it may be the edge of the house, and though you may not break your neck if you walk along the parapet, yet you are best keeping well to this side of it. You are least likely to fall into sin by keeping well away from the edge, and you cannot afford to run risks. Furthermore, let us not give to our children an example which will cause them to run that much closer to the edge. Let us so walk that they may go step by step where we go.

Edited from an article in *The Sword and the Trowel*, August 1869

10
Moving House
Spiritual Observations from Relocation

W E HAVE OFTEN BEEN ADVISED to rise from Nightingale Lane to higher ground, to escape a portion of the fogs and damps which hang almost always over our smoky city. In the good providence of God we have been led to do so, and we are now upon the southern heights. We did not seek out the place, but it came into our hands in a very remarkable manner, and we were bound to accept it. We have left the three-windowed room, which has been so long our study, and the delightful garden where we were wont to walk and meditate. Not without many a regret have we transferred our nest from our dear old home to the Hill of Beulah.

What a type of our departure out of this world is a removal from an abode in which we have lived for years! Many thoughts have thronged our mind while we have been on the wing from the spot where we have dwelt for more than twenty years. Our musings have worked out the parallel between our change and 'the last remove', and here are the notes of it.

On such a day we *must* quit. There is no altering it; we must leave all the dear familiar chambers, and the cosy nooks, and comfortable corners. The matter is settled, and there is no altering it; therefore, take another look round, and prepare to say farewell. Just thus shall it be when the inevitable decree shall go forth, 'Arise ye, and depart; for this is not your rest.' There will be no evasion of the order, no lingering, even for an hour, beyond the time. We are summoned by an authority which must be obeyed.

The warning being given, the dwelling becomes a mere lodging, a place in which we are no more inhabitants, but transient visitors. The whole character of the house is altered, and we ourselves act a different part; the freeholder becomes a temporary tenant, and the child at home changes into an expectant traveller. Were we fully alive to the fact of our approaching death, our position in this body and this world would be far other than it often is; we should no longer regard ourselves as fixtures, but as strangers and sojourners, soon to be removed.

When the actual flitting is near, the furniture begins to be packed up, stores are arranged in cases, and all things are set in marching order. We have scarce a table to eat at, or a chair to sit upon, for we are on the move. So will our last hours call for a setting of the house in order, and a preparing to depart. Small comfort will earthly gear afford us then; in fact, there will remain nothing which we can rest upon, nothing will remain for us. Our hearts must cherish a good hope of a new and better mansion, or they will have a wretched time of it in the hour of departure. We are going, and we leave the dear old house with keen regrets; it would be a pity if we could do other-wise, for it would appear as if we had been unhappy in our abode. It is natural that the soul should be loath to quit the body in which it has resided so long.

For who, to dumb forgetfulness a prey,
This pleasing, anxious being e'er resigned,
Left the warm precincts of this house of clay,
Nor cast one longing, lingering look behind?

The joy of the believer is that he will be no loser by his removal; he has elsewhere a house not made with hands, eternal in the heavens; he will not be houseless, but will enter into his everlasting habitation. Away there, on the hill-tops of glory, stand the mansions which Christ has prepared for them that love him. Shall we dread the hour when we shall take possession of our palace? No, rather let us look forward with joyful expectancy. This, indeed, is a notable part of the removal experience, this looking forward to the new home. Our minds are up and away in the house which we are to occupy for the future, and this takes away regret at leaving the old abode. O to have one's heart and mind in Heaven! Let us already sit in the heavenly places with Christ Jesus, for this he has raised us up together with himself.

Reader, when you have to remove from earth, have you a dwelling-place in Heaven? You are only a tenant at will to the great Lord of all, and you may have notice to quit at any time; if such notice came today, where would you go? Have you ever considered this question? Or will you take a leap in the dark? If you have no mansion above, is it not time you considered your latter end, and the dread alternative of endless joy or misery? A little thought may save a tempest of remorse, therefore sit still a while and consider the world to come. Remember, that both for this world and the next your best friend is Jesus, and that if you trust him he will surely save you. No time can ever be better for the beginning of that trust than this very instant.

From *Spurgeon's Almanack*

11

The Winter Campaign

An insight into the labours of a vast congregation enjoying a time of awakening.
Portions of an exhortation applicable today.

THE NEXT FEW MONTHS ARE, in many churches, the period of harvest when we look for larger meetings. Between this month and the spring much may be accomplished if pastors and churches have a mind to work. The time has come: are we ready to avail ourselves of it? It is important that ministers should call special attention to the usual prayer meetings by mentioning them from the pulpit, with a special request that they may be well attended, or, better still, by a sermon on the topic, stirring up the minds of the members. People's minds are exercised with many thoughts when they see that the pastor is setting himself in a zealous manner to the work of God, and availing himself of the opportunities of the season.

Every one of the members of a congregation should be made to feel – 'Whether I help or hinder, whether I unite in effort or am idle, whether I get a blessing or remain indifferent, the minister in God's name has summoned the church to seek a gracious visitation of the Holy Spirit, and he acts like a man who will not rest without it.'

Then, having cried unto the Lord for strength, the church should each week make some distinct inroad upon the territory of the arch-enemy. We assume that her Sunday Schools, her Bible Classes, her preaching stations, her tract distribution, and so on, are all maintained with vigour, and that grace rests on all the workers. What we have to propose is extra and beyond all this. We suggest some new effort, beyond all that is already done, should be made every week.

For instance, in the department of tract distribution, could not a number of selected tracts be produced at the meeting for prayer, paid for by the gifts of all, and then distributed to all for dissemination all over the district during the week? In large towns, tens of thousands do not even know of the existence of a chapel which may stand within a street or two of them.

Or take another instance of what we may do. Is there room for more children in the Sunday School? Then let the meeting for prayer, at one of its gatherings, consider mainly the School, and plead for a blessing upon it, and let the godly persons there agree to scour the neighbourhood to bring in all the stray children. If the pastor and superintendent would come prepared with a map or plan, with districts marked out, they would probably find sufficient persons volunteering to do all the needful child-gathering, and the whole meeting would feel a far greater interest in the Sunday School than it has ever done before.

Each week, then, we suggest some distinct, new effort for advance, publicly announced and prayed over at the council of war held weekly at the prayer meeting. Real work should be *done*, not talked about.

Meanwhile the congregation should be, by God's help, vigorously plied with the Gospel. Within her own circle – to the very fringe – the church should make it hard for sinners to be at ease. Appeals should not only come from the pastor, but from all the members. Whichever way the unconverted turn they should be confronted with expostulations, entreaties, invitations and warnings. Frequent seasons should be set apart for enquirers: the pastor and officers should lay themselves out to converse with all persons under concern of soul. No one should find it difficult to unbosom his doubts, or relate his struggles after pardon: all experienced believers should be upon the watch to lend their aid. Love on fire with holy zeal must make the meetings pleasing, and induce the timid to take courage, the retiring to be less backward, and the self-condemned to be more at ease in the company of believers.

During this winter crusade a course of sermons upon the first truths of the Gospel would be peculiarly appropriate, and if all hearers were urged to bring friends with them it would be well. At any rate the preacher must dwell largely at this time upon arousing the soul-saving topics. He must preach Jesus most distinctly, and the plan of justification by faith as clearly as words can put it. The more advanced truths can wait awhile, but the rudiments of the Gospel *must* be laid before people's minds in the hope that they will believe and live. Every sermon should have a warm side for sinners, and never be concluded without the proclamation of free grace.

Every believer should be doubly on the alert in watching for souls. None in the congregation should be able to say, 'We attended that place, but no one spoke to us.' If all members of the church became seekers of souls they would, with God's blessing, all become winners of souls. This would yield a season of increase such as our present experience has not enabled us to realise.

O that the Lord would send forth real power into our midst! We need not great talents or intense excitement. With what we already have the battle may be won if the Lord will put his Spirit within us. The ox-goad, the jawbone, the sling-and-stone, and the ram's horn trumpet, have each made an irresistible weapon. With God the instrument is of little importance. His might is everything. Only let us be strong in faith, full of zeal, and very courageous for the Lord our God, and the Lord will bless us. Friends, our marching orders are – FORWARD!

12
Infant Salvation
The Safety of those Dying in Infancy

'Is it well with the child? And she answered, It is well' *(2 Kings 4.26)*.

T HE SHUNAMMITE WOMAN was first asked by Gehazi, whether it was well with herself. She was mourning over a lost child, and yet she said, 'It is well.' She felt that the trial would surely be blessed. Then Gehazi asked, 'Is it well with thy husband?' He was old and stricken in years, and was ripening for death, yet she said, 'Yes, it is well.' Then came the question about her child, which was dead at home, 'Is it well with the child?' Surely this enquiry would renew her grief. Yet she said, 'It is well,' perhaps so answering because she had faith that soon her child would be restored to her, or rather because she was persuaded that whatever might have become of its spirit, it was safe in the keeping of God, happy beneath the shadow of his wings. Therefore, not fearing that it was lost, and having no suspicion whatever that it was cast away from the place of bliss, she said, 'Yes, the child is dead, but it is well.'

Let every mother and father know assuredly that it is well with the child, if God has taken it away from you in its infant days. You never heard its declaration of faith; it was not capable of such a thing. It was not baptised into the Lord Jesus Christ. It was not capable of giving that 'answer of a good conscience toward God'; nevertheless, you may rest assured that it is well with the child, well in a higher and a better sense than it is well with yourselves. The child is 'well' without limitation, without exception, infinitely and eternally.

Perhaps you will say, 'What reasons have we for believing that it is well with the child?' Before I enter upon that I would make one observation. It has been wickedly, lyingly, and slanderously said of Calvinists, that we believe that some little children perish. Those who make the accusation know that their charge is false. I cannot even dare to hope, though I would wish to do so, that they ignorantly misrepresent us. They wickedly repeat what has been denied a thousand times, what they know is not true.

In Calvin's advice to Knox, he interprets the second commandment, 'Shewing mercy unto thousands of them that love me,' as referring to generations, and hence he seems to teach that dying infants who have had believing ancestors, no matter how remotely, are saved. This would certainly take in the whole race.

As for modern Calvinists, I know of no exception, but we all hope and believe that all persons dying in infancy are elect. Dr Gill, who has been looked upon in late times as being a very standard of Calvinism, not to say of ultra-Calvinism, himself never hints for a moment the supposition that any infant has perished. He affirms that it is a dark and mysterious subject, but states that it is his belief, and he thinks he has Scripture to warrant it, that they who have fallen asleep in infancy have not perished but have been numbered with the chosen of God, and so have entered into eternal rest. We have never taught the contrary, and when the charge is brought, I repudiate it and say, 'You may have said so, we never did, and you know we never did.' We have never dreamed of such a thing. With very few and rare exceptions, so rare that I never heard of them except from the lips of slanderers, we have never imagined that infants dying as infants have perished, but we have believed that they enter into the paradise of God.

First, I shall endeavour to explain the way in which we believe infants are saved; secondly, give reasons for so believing; and then, thirdly, seek to bring out a practical use of the subject.

First of all, *the way in which we believe infants to be saved.* Some ground the idea of the eternal blessedness of the infant upon its *innocence.* We do no such thing; we believe that all infants fell in the first Adam, 'For…in Adam all die.' All Adam's posterity, whether infant or adult, were represented by him – he stood for them all, and when he fell, he fell for them all. There was no exception made in the covenant of works made with Adam as to infants dying. Therefore, as they were included in Adam, though they have not sinned after the similitude of Adam's transgression, they *have* original guilt. They are 'born in sin and shapen in iniquity; in sin do their mothers conceive them'. David says this of himself, and (by inference) of the whole human race.

If infants are to be saved, it is not because of any *natural* innocence. They must enter Heaven by the very same way that we do; they must be received in the name of Christ, 'For other foundation can no man lay than that is laid.' There is no different foundation for the infant than that which is laid for the adult.

Equally, it is far from our minds to believe that infants go to Heaven through *baptism.* When children are taught that in their baptism they are made the children of God, and inheritors of the kingdom of Heaven, this is as base a lie as ever was forged in hell, or uttered beneath the canopy of Heaven. Our spirit sinks at the fearful errors which have crept into the church, through the one little door of infant sprinkling. No, children are not saved because they are baptised. The child is saved, if snatched away by death, just as we are.

On what ground, then, do we believe the child to be saved? We believe it to be as lost as the rest of mankind, and as truly condemned by the sentence which said, 'In the day that thou eatest thereof thou shalt surely die.' It is saved because it is *elect*. In the compass of election, in the Lamb's book of life, we believe there shall be found written millions of souls who are only shown briefly on earth, and then stretch their wings for Heaven.

They are saved, too, because they were *redeemed* by the precious blood of Jesus Christ. He who shed his blood for all his people, bought those dying in infancy with the same price with which he redeemed their parents, and therefore are they saved because Christ was Sponsor for them, and suffered in their stead.

They are saved, also, by *regeneration*, for, 'except a man' – the text does not mean exclusively an adult man, but a being of the human race – 'except a man be born again, he cannot see the kingdom of God.' No doubt, in some mysterious manner the Spirit of God regenerates the infant soul, so that it enters into glory made meet to be a partaker of the inheritance of the saints in light. That such regeneration is possible is proved from Scripture. John the Baptist was filled with the Holy Spirit from his mother's womb. We believe, therefore, that even before the intellect can work, God, by the mysterious agency of his Holy Spirit, may create the infant soul a new creature in Christ Jesus, enabling it to enter into the rest which remaineth for the people of God. By election, redemption and regeneration, the child enters into glory. If we did not suppose that dying infants were saved in the same way as adults, it would be necessary to suppose that God's justice could be set aside, and that his plan of salvation could be altered to suit their case.

Secondly, *the reasons why we thus think infants are saved*. We ground our conviction about infant salvation very much upon the *goodness of the nature of God*. We say that the opposite doctrine that some infants perish and are lost, is altogether repugnant to the idea which we have of him whose name is Love. If we had a god whose name was Moloch; if God were an arbitrary tyrant, without benevolence or grace, we could imagine some infants being cast into hell. But our God, who heareth the young ravens when they cry, certainly will find no delight in the shrieks and cries of infants cast away from his presence. We read of God that he is so tender that he would not have the mouth of the ox muzzled when treading out the corn. He cares for the bird upon the nest, and would not have the mother bird killed while sitting upon its nest with its little ones. He made ordinances and commands even to protect irrational creatures.

Shall we believe with such universal goodness as his, that he would cast away the infant soul? I say it would be so contrary to all that we have ever read or ever believed of him, that our faith would stagger before a revelation which should display a fact so singularly exceptional to the tenor of his other deeds. We have learned humbly to submit our judgements to his will, and we dare not criticise or accuse the Lord of all. He is just; let him do as he may! Whatever he reveals we will accept! But he never has, and I think he never will, require of us so desperate a stretch of faith as to see *goodness* in the eternal misery of an infant cast into hell.

You remember when Jonah – petulant, quick-tempered Jonah – would have Nineveh perish, God gave as the reason why Nineveh should not be destroyed, that there were more than six-score thousand infants – persons who knew not their right hand from their left. If he spared Nineveh that their mortal life might be spared, do we think that their immortal souls shall be needlessly cast away?

Again, we think that eternal banishment of those dying in infancy would be utterly inconsistent with *the known character of our Lord Jesus Christ*. When his disciples put away the little children whom their anxious mothers brought to him, Jesus said, 'Suffer little children, and forbid them not, to come unto me: for of such is the kingdom of heaven.' By this he taught, as John Newton very properly says, that such children made up a very great part of the kingdom of Heaven.

When we consider that upon the best statistics it is calculated that more than one third of the human race die in infancy, and probably half the population of the world, if we take into calculation those districts where infanticide prevails, the saying of the Saviour derives great force indeed – 'of such is the kingdom of heaven'.

If some remind me that the kingdom of Heaven means the dispensation of grace on earth, I answer, yes, it does, and it means the same dispensation in Heaven too. Our Lord's words prove that infants compose a great part of his family, and that he has a love and amiableness towards the little ones. When they shouted in the temple, 'Hosanna!' did he rebuke them? On the contrary he rejoiced in their shouts. Then he declared: 'Out of the mouth of babes and sucklings thou hast perfected praise.' And does not that text seem to say that in Heaven there shall be *perfect praise* rendered to God by multitudes who were here on earth – your little ones suddenly snatched away to Heaven?

I could not believe it of Jesus, that he would say to little children, 'Depart from me, ye cursed, into everlasting fire in hell!' I cannot conceive it possible for him as the loving and tender One, that when he shall sit to judge all nations, he should put the little ones on the left hand, and should banish them for ever from his presence. Could he address *them*, and say to them, 'I was an hungred, and ye gave me no meat: I was thirsty, and ye gave me no drink…sick, and in prison, and ye visited me not?' How *could* they have treated him so? And if the main reason for damnation lies in sins of omission like these, which it was not possible for them to commit (for lack of power to perform the duty) how, then, shall he condemn and cast them away?

Furthermore, we think that *the ways of grace*, if we consider them, render it highly improbable (if not impossible) that infant souls should be destroyed. 'What saith the scripture?' We know that God is so abundantly gracious from such expressions as: 'The unsearchable riches of Christ'; 'God, who is rich in mercy'; 'A God full of compassion'; 'The exceeding riches of his grace'. All these are truly applicable without exaggeration or hyperbole. We know that God is good to all, and his tender mercies are over all his works. The grace of God has sought out the greatest sinners in the world. It has not passed by the vilest of the vile. He who called himself the chief of sinners was a partaker of the love of Christ.

All manner of sin and of blasphemy have been forgiven unto man. God has been able to save unto the uttermost them that come unto him by Christ, and does it seem consistent with such grace as this that it should altogether pass by the myriads upon myriads of little ones, who wear the image of the earthy Adam, and yet never receive the image of the heavenly? I cannot conceive such a thing. He that has tasted, and felt, and handled the grace of God, will, I think, shrink instinctively from any other doctrine than this, that infants dying as such, are most assuredly saved.

Once again, one of the strongest inferential arguments is to be found in the fact that Scripture positively states that the number of saved souls at the last will be very great. In *Revelation* we read of a great multitude which no man can number. The psalmist speaks of them as numerous as dew drops from the womb of the morning. Many passages give to Abraham, as the father of the faithful, a seed as many as the stars of heaven, or as the sand on the seashore. The virtue of precious redemption involves a great host who were redeemed. All Scripture seems to teach that Heaven will not be a narrow world, that its population will not be like a handful gleaned out of a vintage, but that Christ shall be glorified by ten thousand times ten thousand whom he hath redeemed with his blood.

Now where are all these to come from? How small a part of the map could be called Christian! Look at it. Out of that part which could be called Christian, how small a portion of them would bear the name of believer! How few could be said to have even a nominal attachment to the Church of Christ. Out of those who *do* name the name of Christ, how many are hypocrites, and know not the Truth!

I do not see it possible that so vast a number should enter Heaven, unless it be on the supposition that infant souls constitute the great majority.

It is a sweet belief to my own mind that there will be more saved than lost, for in all things Christ is to have the pre-eminence, and why not in this? It was the thought of a great divine that perhaps at the last, the number of the lost would not bear a greater proportion to the number of the saved, than do the number of criminals in gaols to those who are abroad in a properly conducted state. I hope it may be found to be so. I do know that Christ will have the victory, and that as he is followed by streaming hosts, the black prince of hell will never be able to count so many followers in *his* dreary train as Christ in his resplendent triumph. And if so, we *must* have the children saved. Chiefly though, we must have them because we feel anyhow they must be numbered with the blessed, and dwell with Christ hereafter.

Now for one or two incidental matters which occur in Scripture which seem to throw a little light also on the subject. We must not forget the case of David. His child by Bathsheba was to die as a punishment for the father's offence. David prayed and fasted and vexed his soul, but at last they told him the child was dead. He fasted no more, but he said, 'I shall go to him, but he shall not return to me.' Now, where did David expect to go to? Why, to Heaven surely. Then his child must have been there, for he said, 'I shall go to him.' I do not hear him say the same of Absalom. He did not stand over his corpse and say, 'I shall go to him.' He had no hope for that rebellious son. Over this child it was not – 'O my son!…would God I had died for thee!' No, he could let this babe go with perfect confidence, for he said, 'I shall go to him.' He might have said, 'I know that he hath made with me an everlasting covenant, ordered in all things and sure, and when I walk through the valley of the shadow of death I shall fear no evil, for he is with me. I shall go to my child, and in Heaven we shall be reunited with each other.'

Then you have the passage, 'Out of the mouth of babes and suck-lings thou hast perfected praise.' The coming out of Egypt was a type of the redemption of the chosen seed, and you know that in that case the little ones were to go forth. Why should not children in the greater deliverance join in the song of Moses and of the Lamb?

In *Ezekiel 16.21* God censures his people for having given up their little infants to Moloch, having caused them to pass through the fire, and he says of these little ones, 'Thou hast slain *my* chil-dren, and delivered them to cause them to pass through the fire.' So, then, they were *God's* children while babes. We may therefore believe concerning all those who have fallen asleep in these early days of life, that Jesus said of them, 'These are *my* children.' He still carries the lambs in his bosom, as Isaiah says.

There is another passage in Scripture which may be used to show that the sin of the parents shall not necessarily be the ruin of their children. In the first chapter of *Deuteronomy* there had been a threat-ening pronounced upon the children of Israel in the wilderness, that, with the exception of Caleb and Joshua, they should never see the promised land. Nevertheless, it is added, 'Your little ones, which ye said should be a prey, and your children, which in that day had no knowledge between good and evil, they shall go in thither, and unto them will I give it, and they shall possess it.'* Inasmuch as the sin of the generation in the wilderness did not shut the next generation out of Canaan, so the sin of unbelieving parents shall not necessarily be the ruin of their children, but they shall still, through God's sover-eign grace and his overflowing mercy, be made partakers of the rest which he hath reserved for his people.

Note that I have not made a distinction between the children of

---

* In this case the children entered the promised land after growing to adult-hood, but this passage in two ways supports the salvation of infants. First, it conveys the gracious attitude of God to those who are too young to discern good and evil, and secondly it may be seen as 'typical' of infants in relation to the eternal kingdom.

godly and ungodly parents. If they die in infancy, I do not mind who is their father nor who is their mother, they are saved. I certainly do not endorse the theory of a Presbyterian minister who supposes that the children of godly parents will have a better place in Heaven than those who happen to be sprung from ungodly ones. I do not believe in any such thing. All of them without exception, from whosesoever loins they may have sprung, will, we believe, not by baptism, not by their parents' faith, but simply as we are all saved through the election of God, through the precious blood of Christ, through the regenerating influence of the Holy Spirit, attain to glory and immortality, and wear the image of the heavenly as they have worn the image of the earthy.

I now come to make *a practical use of this doctrine*. First, let it be a comfort to bereaved parents. You say it is a heavy cross that you have to carry. To have a living cross is indeed a tribulation – to have a child who is rebellious in his childhood, vicious in his youth, debauched in his manhood! Many a parent has been brought with sorrow to the grave through *living* children, but never through dead babes, certainly not if they were Christians and they were able to take the comfort of the apostle's words – 'Ye sorrow not, even as others which have no hope.'

Do you know from what sorrows your little one has escaped? You have had enough yourself. It was born of woman; it might have been full of trouble as you are. It has escaped those sorrows; do you lament that? Remember, too, your own sins, and the deep sorrow of repentance. Had the child lived, it would have been a sinner, and it would have known the bitterness of conviction of sin. It has escaped that and rejoices now in the glory of God.

Bereaved parents, could you for a moment see your own offspring above I think you would very speedily wipe away your tears. You might not have murmured had you received the promise that your child should have been elevated to the peerage; it has been elevated higher than that – to the peerage of Heaven. It has received the dignity of the immortals. It is robed in better than royal garments. It is more rich and more blessed than it could have been if all the crowns of earth could have been put upon its head. How can you complain? An old poet has penned a verse well fitted for an infant's epitaph:

> Short was my life, the longer is my rest;
> God takes those soonest whom he loveth best,
> Who's born today, and dies tomorrow,
> Loses some hours of joy, but months of sorrow.
> Other diseases often come to grieve us,
> Death strikes but once, and that stroke doth relieve us.

Your child has had that one stroke and has been relieved from all these pains, and you may say that it is supremely blessed having escaped from sin and care and woe, and with the Saviour rests. 'Happy the babe,' says Hervey, 'who –

> Privileged by faith, a shorter labour and a lighter weight,
> Received but yesterday the gift of breath,
> Ordered tomorrow to return to death.'

Another, looking upward to the skies, says –

> O blest exchange, O envied lot,
>   Without a conflict crowned,
> Stranger to pain, in pleasure blessed
>   And without fame, renowned.

It is well to sing the song of triumph after we have passed the Red Sea with all its terrors; but to sing the song without the sea is glorious also! I do not know that I would prefer the lot of a child in Heaven myself. I think it is nobler to have borne the storm, and to have struggled against the wind and the rain. I think it will be a subject of congratulation through eternity, for you and me, that we did not come so easy a way to Heaven, for it is only a pin's prick after all, this mortal life; then there is exceeding great glory hereafter.

But yet I think we may still thank God for those little ones, that they have been spared our sins, and spared our infirmities, and spared our pains, and are entered into the rest above. Thus saith the Lord unto Rachel, weeping for her children and refusing to be comforted because they were no more – 'Refrain thy voice from weeping, and thine eyes from tears: for thy work shall be rewarded, saith the Lord; and they shall come again from the land of the enemy.'

What shall we say to parents who have children who live? We have spoken of those that are dead; what shall we say of the living? I think I might say, reserve your tears, bereaved parents, for the children that live. You may go to the little grave. You may look upon it and say, 'This my child is saved; it rests for ever beyond all fear of harm.' Then come back to those who are sitting round your table, and look from one to the other and say, 'Some of these are unsaved.' They do not know God, and some are ripening into manhood and into woman-hood. It is plain to see that their hearts are like every natural heart, desperately wicked. There is subject for weeping for you. I pray that you never cease to weep for them until they have ceased to sin. Never cease to hope for them until they have ceased to live. Never cease to pray for them until you yourself cease to breathe.

Carry them before God in the arms of faith, and do not be despondent because they are not what you want them to be. They will be won yet if you have faith in God. Do not think that it is hopeless. He that saved *you* can save *them*. Take them one by one constantly to God's mercy-seat and wrestle with him, and say, 'I will not let thee go, except thou bless me.'

Pray, strive, wrestle, and it shall yet be your happy lot to see your household saved. This was the word which the apostle gave to the gaoler, 'Believe on the Lord Jesus Christ, and thou shalt be saved, and thy house.' We have had many proofs of it, for in this pool under here I have baptised not only the father and the mother, but in many cases all the children too, when one after another they have been brought by grace to put their trust in Jesus.

It should be the longing of every parent's heart to see all the children as Christ's, and numbered in the host of those who shall sing around the throne of God. We may pray in faith, for we have a promise about it. We may pray in faith, for we have many precedents in Scripture; the God of Abraham is the God of Isaac and the God of Jacob; but for this good thing he will be enquired of by the house of Israel to do it for them. Plead with him, go before him with the power of faith and earnestness, and he will surely hear you.

One word to all. A little child was saying the other day – children say strange things – 'Papa, I cannot go back again.' When he was asked what he meant, he explained that he was here, he had begun his life, and it had occurred to him that he could not *cease* to be. He could not go back again. You and I may say the same. Here we are; we have grown up; we cannot go back again to that childhood in which we once were. We have therefore no door of escape there. We cannot any longer be saved as dying infants.

Good John Bunyan used to wish that he had died when he was a child. Later he hoped he might be descended from some Jew, for he had a notion that the Hebrews might be saved. That door God has closed. Every door is closed to you and me except the one that is just in front of us, and that has the mark of the cross upon it. There is the golden knocker of prayer: do we choose to turn aside from that to find another – a gate of ceremonies, or of blood, or of birth? We shall never enter that way. There is only one true knocker! By faith I will lift it now. 'I, the chief of sinners am, have mercy upon me!' Jesus stands there. 'Come in,' saith he, and receives us to his arms, washes, clothes, glorifies us, when we come to him. Am I such a fool that I do not knock?

And now, sinner, in the name of him that liveth and was dead, and is alive for evermore, lay hold upon that knocker, lift it, and let your prayer be, 'God be merciful to me a sinner!'

Abridged from a sermon preached on 29th September 1861

13

God Uses His People in Soulwinning

'And when he thus had spoken, he cried with a loud voice, Lazarus, come forth. And he that was dead came forth, bound hand and foot with graveclothes: and his face was bound about with a napkin. Jesus saith unto them, Loose him, and let him go' *(John 11.43, 44)*.

IN MANY THINGS OUR LORD JESUS stands alone as a worker. No other can unite his voice with the fiat which says, 'Lazarus, come forth.' Yet in certain points of gracious operation the Master associates his servants with him, so that when Lazarus has come forth he says to them, 'Loose him, and let him go.' In the raising of the dead he is alone, and therein majestic and divine. In the loosing of the bound he is associated with them. In this he remains majestic, but his more prominent feature is condescension. How exceedingly kind it is of our Lord Jesus to permit his disciples to do some little thing in connection with his great deeds, so that they may be 'workers together with him'.

Our Lord as frequently as possible associated his disciples with himself. Of course, they could not aid him in presenting an atoning sacrifice, yet it was their honour that they had said, 'Let us also go, that we may die with him,' and that in their love they resolved to go with him to prison and to death. Our Lord understood the fickleness of their character, yet he knew that they were sincere in their desire to be associated with him in all his life story whatever it might be. Hence, when he afterwards rode into Jerusalem in triumph, he alone was saluted with hosannas; but he sent two of his disciples to bring the ass on which he rode, and they cast their garments upon the colt and they set Jesus thereon, and as he went they spread their clothes in the way. Thus they contributed to his lowly pomp, and shared in the exultation of the royal day.

Further on, when he would keep the feast, he expressly dwells upon it that he would keep it with them; for he said, 'With desire I have desired to eat this passover with you before I suffer.' He sent Peter and John to prepare that passover; he directed them to the large upper room furnished, and there he bade them make ready. Anything that they could do they were allowed to do. Their Lord was willing to have led them further still; but through weakness they stopped short. In the garden he bade them watch with him on that dreadful night, and he sought sympathy from them,

> Backward and forward, thrice he ran,
> As if he sought some help from man.

He cried in sorrowful disappointment, 'Could ye not watch with me one hour?' Ah, no! They could go to the brink of the abyss with him, but they could not descend into its deeps. He must tread the winepress alone, and of the people there must be none with him. Yet as far as they could go he disdained not their dear society. He allowed them according to their capacity to drink of his cup, and to be baptised with his baptism. If their fellowship with him in his sufferings went no farther, it was not because he warned them back, but because they had not the strength to follow. According to his own judgement they were intimately associated with him, for he said to them, 'Ye are they which have continued with me in my temptations.'

Beloved, our Jesus Christ still delights to associate us with him as far as our feebleness and folly will permit. In his present work of bringing sinners to himself, he counts it a part of his reward that we should be labourers together with him. In his working people he beholds the travail of his soul as well as in the sinners whom they bring to him. Thus, he has a double reward, and is as much glorified in the love, and pity, and zeal of his servants as in the harvest which they reap.

As a father smiles to see his little children imitating him, and endeavouring to assist him in his work, so is Jesus pleased to see our lowly efforts for his honour. It is his joy to see the eyes which he has opened weeping with him over the impenitent, and to hear the tongue which he has loosed speaking in prayer and in the preaching of the Gospel. It is his joy to see any of the members he has restored and healed occupied as members of righteousness in his service. Jesus Christ is glad to save sinners at all, but most of all glad to save them by the means of those already saved.

Thus he blesses the prodigal sons and the servants of the household at the same moment. He gives to the lost salvation, and upon his own called and chosen ones he puts the honour of being used for the grandest purposes under Heaven. It is more honourable to save a soul from death than to rule an empire. Such honour all the saints may have.

From a sermon preached 20th April 1884

14

Taking Care of Others
The Innkeeper in the Parable of the Good Samaritan

'But a certain Samaritan, as he journeyed, came where he was: and when he saw him, he had compassion on him, and went to him, and bound up his wounds, pouring in oil and wine, and set him on his own beast, and brought him to an inn, and took care of him. And on the morrow when he departed, he took out two pence, and gave them to the host, and said unto him, Take care of him; and whatsoever thou spendest more, when I come again, I will repay thee' *(Luke 10.33-35).*

WHEN THE SAVIOUR SPOKE, he spoke volumes. We take a little bit of his gold and hammer it out into acres of gold leaf, and we do well in so doing, for we cannot talk ingots of gold as he did. His words were pearls and rubies and diamonds, and often they meant not only the finite meaning which we can put into practice, but infinite meanings which only he can fulfil. We shall be wise if we carefully weigh his sentences.

I am going to throw a sidelight on the parable. It is not the direct teaching of the parable, but it is a gleam of latent light on another subject. What our Saviour taught us to be, he was. When, therefore, he described the good Samaritan, he pictured himself, for to us he has acted the good Samaritan. What he has commanded us to do in this parable, he has himself done, for he is our example as well as our teacher. This is my first head, and after it I shall briefly touch upon four more points.

1 The Lord's example

This Samaritan, we are told, took care of the injured man. *Christ has taken great care of wounded souls.* The Samaritan brought him to an inn, and took care of him. I will not dwell upon it at length. I think you understand it. You too were wounded once and you have not forgotten it. You were sore wounded; it seemed as if all sorrows had met in you, and all because you discovered that you had sinned.

Personal sin is a dread discovery when a person has really made it for himself. It is not much to say, 'I have sinned.' It is not much to believe the fact that you have sinned. But to find it coming home to you; your sins clinging to you like so much burning pitch cleaving to your skin; even worse, your sins within you pricking your conscience so that you cannot rest day or night – this is terrible! You feel anxious to flee, but know not where. We did not all pass through this state of mind to the same degree, but, more or less, each child of God knows what this means. We find ourselves wounded, bleeding, faint, and dying, with no power to help ourselves, and no friend near who could succour us!

You recollect all that; and in that hour Jesus came by. I think I see him now as first I saw him when I looked to him – so tender in his looks! He came where I was, stopped at the sight of me, stooped over me, and bade me trust myself with him, for he would handle me most tenderly. I did so. What could I do better than just leave myself with him? I think I see him now, looking at my wounds, washing them, pouring in the oil and wine, then binding them and strapping them about. Never was there such a surgeon. I felt my life returning to me at his every touch; at his every look and breath; and, more, I felt a strange realisation creeping over me that made me know that, somehow, I was new – was, in fact, born again, and had passed from death unto life.

The first perception of that fact is with me still; it was no dream or passing enthusiasm. That day is as fresh to me as if it were yesterday. The snow was falling fast, yet ten thousand winged doves seemed to come flying out of Heaven to meet me on my way, for I was at peace with God. I had to tell out my joy. I had to tell it straightaway. I could not hold it in: the joy was too great for silence. Christ Jesus had done it. He had made a miserable heart glad in a moment. He had taken away my sackcloth, and girded me with gladness; taken away the ashes on my miserable head, and set there a coronet of joyous hope. He did it all. He took great care of me. I want you that know all about his love to supplement my story by saying, 'Yes, that is what he did with me. He took care of me.' My Lord sat up with me at nights, and when I woke up in the morning, what encouraging things he put into my mind! Yes, and he followed me when I had to go about the world, and was likely to be tempted. He took care of me.

My boyish sports might have brought temptations, and my mixing with other youths might have brought me into evil; but he took care of me. Looking back upon my first days of conversion I bear witness that he really took care of me. And because of this *I am bound to take care of others.* Do you not feel the same?

2 The Lord's command

Secondly, *Jesus in his absence would have his church take care of wounded souls.* He – 'brought him to an inn, and took care of him. And on the morrow when he departed, he took out two pence, and gave them to the host, and said unto him, Take care of him.'

Jesus Christ has brought many a wounded soul to his church, and his order is, 'Take care of him.' For this purpose is the church instituted, that you may have the cure and care of souls. You who just now were agreeing that Christ took care of *you*, must now hear him say of another, 'Take care of him.'

It is my special office to take care of all the sick souls who come to this great caravanserai;* but I cannot do this unless you all help me. Some of my friends look round the Tabernacle to find out the wounded ones, speak with them, and so take care of them. Alas, even many church members come in and out, and never think about others; but this must not be so any longer! Jesus says to his church, as to the host of an inn, 'Take care of him,' for in a sick soul there are *wounds* which need much care. They are not easily healed, these wounds of the heart. They bleed afresh, even when you think that you have healed them.

Some minds are so terribly bruised on account of past sin that they will never come to a permanent healing so that they can rejoice in the Lord and serve him, unless *you* take special care of them. We have around us despondent ones who will not get into light and liberty unless we take care of them by instruction and consolation.

How we must care

Besides wounds, they suffer from weaknesses. A man cannot be beaten and bruised and left half dead, without being very weak. Take care of him then. Let us look out for Little-Faiths, and Much-Afraids, and Feeble-Minds; and lay ourselves out to strengthen them. When we find them, let us not despise them. Let us not seek out more congenial company, and avoid the feeble and despondent; but let us converse with them, that we may take care of them. After we have healed their wounds, and bound up their broken bones, let us continue to nurse them, and give them food suitable to their sick state. Would God that a tenth part of the care which some Christians show towards their horses [*nowadays their cars*] and their dogs were

---

* Eastern quadrangular inn with huge inner court for caravans of merchants or pilgrims.

exercised upon Christ's beloved ones whom he commits to our charge, and of whom he says, pointing them out one by one – 'Take care of him!'

When wounds are healed, weakness is removed and hunger is satisfied, he who acts as Christ's host will discover that the needy man has no adequate clothing. We are told that this poor man had been stripped of his raiment. Supposing the host had said, 'I have doctored you up so that you can walk; and now you may go.' He might have answered, 'How can I go? I have lost my clothes.' Then would come to the host's mind the word of the good Samaritan, 'Take care of him' – which included – 'Clothe him.' So let us endeavour, as much as we can, to clothe every renewed soul with the garments of salvation. Let us so teach, instruct, and console, that those who come to us naked shall go forth from us with the robes of joy, comfort, and strength wrapped about them, to take their journey to the New Jerusalem in fit apparel. In all things we must see that the man of God be thoroughly furnished for his heavenward journey.

Nor is this all. The succoured pilgrim says, 'I am going on my journey, and I am thankful for what you have done for me. But when I started out from home, I had bread in my pack, and money in my pocket, with which to pay the charges of the way. Alas, I am now penniless!' Then the host would say to him, 'He that brought you here said, "Take care of him," and I must interpret his words very liberally, for he is of a generous mind. Here is money to pay your charges till you reach your home.'

Let us never relinquish the care of a soul till it is safely housed in Heaven. Take care of one another, but especially let those who are strong take great care of the weak. Some will want to be cared for throughout all the way. I am occupied, in my small way, just as Mr Greatheart was employed in Bunyan's day. I do not compare myself with that champion, but I am in the same line of business. I am employed in personally-conducted tours to Heaven, and I have with me, at the present time, dear Old Father Honest: I am glad he is still alive and active. And there is Christiana, and here are her children. It is my business, as best I can, to kill dragons, and cut off giants' heads, and lead the timid and trembling.

Care all the way

I am often afraid of losing some of the weaklings. I have much heartache for them, but by God's grace, and with your kind and generous help in looking after one another, I hope we shall all travel safely to the river's edge. Oh, how many have I had to part with there! I have stood on the brink, and I have heard their singing in the midst of the stream, and I have almost seen the shining ones lead them up the hill into the celestial city. That is my line of business. My Lord has said to me, 'Take care of him.' I want many of you to share in this happy work, for our dear Master's sake. He has gone away, but he has left sick souls in our charge. Let us take great care of them.

3 The Lord's provision

Thirdly, I have to note to you that *our Lord has provided for these sick ones*. We read of the good Samaritan that 'he took out two pence, and gave them to the host'. Two pence then meant a great deal more than two pence would mean in these times. Two pence was a considerable sum in those days, and would defray the charges of such simple living as they had at oriental caravanserais for a considerable time.

Now the Master has given to many of you these two pence to pay the charges of sick ones for some time to come. What a sum we have in hand in the means of grace! The preaching of the Word: what a help it is to the wounded, the sick, and the weary! The writing and scattering of sound religious books is another way of nourishing those who are committed to our charge. The ordinance of baptism, and especially the ordinance of the Lord's Supper – the Master has given us these things as spending money for the hospitalities of his church. 'There,' says he, 'use these. Use these, that you may find in them sufficient for taking care of the wounded and weak.'

Another piece of spending money that he has given us is the benefit of Christian fellowship. You and I know that it is one of the sweetest things outside of Heaven to talk to one another, and to exchange notes of our experience. As nations are enriched by commerce, so are Christians enriched by communion. As we exchange commodities in trade, so do we exchange our different forms of knowledge while we speak to one another of the things of the kingdom. The Saviour has given us this Christian fellowship to be as it were the two pence to defray the charges of those whom he has entrusted to our care. In what he has left as a legacy to the church he has left us ample means to go on with. We have not spent the two pence yet in any one case.

4 Special cases

But fourthly, I now call to your notice that *there may be some persons with whom there may be greater expenses than usual.* 'There,' says the Master, 'there are the two pence; but if anything more be needed, spend it, and I will repay thee.' Some will need more than preaching; more than ordinances. What sort are these?

Some are more than ordinarily injured. They have long lived in sin. Their conviction of sin is very terrible. You cannot make them well on the usual expenditure of two pence. The ordinary means will not reach their desperate cases. Do not despair, but go on, and spend more. Do more for them than you would do for the rest of the sick and wounded who lodge at the church's inn.

Some are more than ordinarily weak. There is Miss Much-Afraid. Sometimes when I talk with her I leave her in a comfortable frame, and I hope she will be no more sad. Alas, she is just as much afraid tomorrow! Mr Feeble-Mind – do you not know him? You sometimes get a little out of patience with the brother because he is so very weak. Let us be doubly tender to his feebleness, and spend on him more than we should like to lay out on all comers. The Good Samaritan who put them under our care, has said, 'If you spend more, when I come again, I will repay you.' Let us not stint these needy ones, for the Lord would not be pleased if we did.

Many are not only more wounded, and more weak, but they are more dull of comprehension. Some flesh is hard to heal; some minds find it very hard to receive consolation. It takes a long time to get a Gospel notion into certain people's heads.

Martin Luther talked of beating the heads of the Wittenbergers with the Book to get justification by faith into their brains. But beating is of no use. We must spend much more than twopenny-worth of patience on them. We must repeat over, and over, and over again the elements of Truth. It must be, 'Precept upon precept, precept upon precept; line upon line, line upon line; here a little, and there a little.' If any require more trouble and patience than others, we must spend it on them freely.

Some are *more desperately tried than others.* We wonder why some men do not make better Christians than they do. Ah, you do not know their wives! You wonder why some women do not make brighter Christians. You do not know their husbands! You wonder that yonder dear child, who showed such bright early tokens of grace, did not grow into a fine man. You do not know the example he had at home! Oh, if we could follow many of our dear brothers and sisters back to the rooms which they are forced to call 'homes' and see what they have to see, and hear what they have to hear, we would not be astonished that they need a great deal of care! But the Master says to us, 'Take care of them. See them through. Never be weary of them.'

Lastly, some of these people are lamentably trying. I know persons whom I love very much, and hope to see in Heaven, but they are a sad trial to me now. All of you who work for the Lord must have fallen in with good people who are a living cross to all around them. Ill temper, obstinacy, changeableness, singularity, each one will produce a character hard to put up with; but we are bound to bear with them all to the end. When we have gone as far as the customary two pence, we must not stop, but spend on. Our Lord seems to say, 'Run up a bill: put no limit to your spiritual expense; for whatsoever thou spendest more, when I come again, I will repay thee.'

5 The reward of the Lord

With that I am going to finish – *for those who want more care than usual, we shall be rewarded when the Lord comes.* 'When I come again, I will repay thee.' This reminds us that he will come again. He is on the road. He may be here very soon; and when he comes again he will repay us. Think of his ever being in our debt! Imagine his asking us to let it stand over till he comes again!

I have been turning this over in my mind, and I can hardly accept it. A dear friend did me a great kindness in a difficult matter. It was in his line of business, and when I saw him, I said, 'You will send in your bill, please.' He said, 'You will pay it when I send it in.' A month or two passed away, and I wrote to him, telling him that I was never in anybody's debt, and I did not like to leave an account outstanding. Would he send me his bill? He only said, 'Yes, yes: you will pay it when I send it in.' I worried him to send the bill, and at length said, 'I must have it.' Then he sent it in, and put down his charge in full, but across a stamp at the bottom he had written, 'Settled by love'.

When my Master says to me, 'When I come again, I will repay thee,' I reply, 'It is already settled by love.' In fact, it was settled long ago. We owe him so much that it is impossible that he can ever owe us anything that would need to be booked. Dear friends, if you will look after the Lord's poor wounded ones, he says, 'I will repay you.' You have an 'I-O-U' from your Lord. Jesus is such a liberal paymaster that we are glad to wait as long as he pleases. The interest which he gives is beyond measure. He pays ten thousand percent on all that he owes; and we are therefore willing to let the 'debt' keep on running as long as he pleases. Let us henceforth grudge nothing, but spend with all our might upon the wounded ones whom Jesus brings to our door. Beloved, this is a short sermon, but it will take you long to carry it out in practice.

Written for *The Sword and the Trowel* in 1888

www.MetropolitanTabernacle.org

The Metropolitan Tabernacle is a large congregation in central London proclaiming the Gospel of salvation and the doctrines of grace.

See website for details of services, *Sword & Trowel* magazine, seminary, other ministries, and free video/audio sermon downloads.

The Suffering Letters
of C. H. Spurgeon
155 pages, illustrated paperback, ISBN 978 1 870855 60 0

These remarkable letters, written from a suffering pastor to his congregation, abound in exhortations to godliness, zeal and prayer. They provide a unique insight into Spurgeon's life, and into the fervent soul-winning activity which was, alongside the preaching, a leading feature of an historic Calvinistic church.

Notes on Spurgeon's ministry set the letters in context, and several classic sermonettes written during sickness are included, along with 16 pages of colour pictures of original letters.

Faith, Doubts, Trials and Assurance
Peter Masters

139 pages, paperback, ISBN 978 1 870855 50 1

Ongoing faith is essential for answered prayer, effective service, spiritual stability and real communion with God. In this book many questions are answered about faith, such as –

How may we assess the state of our faith?
How can faith be strengthened?
How should difficult doubts be handled?
How can we tell if troubles are intended to chastise or to refine?
What can be done to obtain assurance?
Can a believer commit the unpardonable sin?
Exactly how is the Lord's presence felt?

The author provides answers, with much pastoral advice, drawing on Scripture throughout.

The Faith
Great Christian Truths
Peter Masters

119 pages, paperback, ISBN 978 1 870855 54 9

There is nothing like this popular, non-technical sweep through key themes of the Christian faith, highlighting very many inspiring and enlivening points. It often takes an unusual approach to a topic in order to bring out the full wonder and significance.

It is designed to be enjoyed by seasoned Christians, and also by all who want to explore the great features of the faith, and discover the life of the soul.

CONTENTS:

The Mysterious Nature of a Soul	The New Birth
What God is Actually Like	Why the Resurrection?
The Fall of Man	Prophecies of Resurrection
The Three Dark Hours of Calvary	The Holy Trinity

Classic Counsels
C. H. Spurgeon
126 pages, paperback, ISBN 978 1 870855 42 6

These choice messages cover aspects of personal spiritual experience together with Christian responsibilities, in Spurgeon's distinctively compelling and uplifting style.

Topics include: obtaining assurance, help for doubting seekers, relief for the downcast believer, mature faith and how it is reached, the Christian and places of entertainment, counsel for witnessing Christians, safety for seeking souls, a call to prayer meetings and the immense significance of a believer.

Selected from sermons and shorter addresses, some given to the Tabernacle Prayer Meeting, these edited messages have been slightly abridged, and punctuation has been modernised.

Steps for Guidance
In the Journey of Life
Peter Masters

134 pages, paperback, ISBN 978 1 870855 66 2

In recent years the subject of how to find God's guidance has become controversial. Some say that God does not have a specific plan for the lives of his people, but allows us to please ourselves. Others say God's will is known by dreams, visions, and 'words of knowledge'.

By contrast with these sadly unbiblical ideas, this book presents the time-honoured, scriptural view that Christians must seek God's will in all the major decisions of life, such as career, marriage, location, and church. Six essential steps are traced from the Bible, and principles are given on additional practical issues such as possessions and leisure activities; ambition and wealth; joining or leaving a church.

Not Like Any Other Book
Peter Masters

161 pages, paperback, ISBN 978 1 870855 43 3

Faulty Bible interpretation lies at the root of every major mistake and 'ism' assailing churches today, and countless Christians are asking for the old, traditional and proven way of handling the Bible to be spelled out plainly.

A new approach to interpretation has also gripped many evangelical seminaries and Bible colleges, an approach based on the ideas of unbelieving critics, stripping the Bible of God's message, and leaving pastors impoverished in their preaching.

This book reveals what is happening, providing many brief examples of right and wrong interpretation. The author shows that the Bible includes its own rules of interpretation, and every believer should know what these are.

For other Wakeman titles please see www.wakemantrust.org